T0354850

Tea with the Midnight Muse

INVOCATIONS & INQUIRIES FOR AWAKENING

SHILOH SOPHIA

BALBOA.
PRESS
A DIVISION OF HAY HOUSE

Balboa Press books may be ordered through booksellers or by contacting:

Balboa Press
A Division of Hay House
1663 Liberty Drive
Bloomington, IN 47403
www.balboapress.com
1 (877) 407-4847

Because of the dynamic nature of the Internet, any web addresses or links contained in this book may have changed since publication and may no longer be valid. The views expressed in this work are solely those of the author and do not necessarily reflect the views of the publisher, and the publisher hereby disclaims any responsibility for them.

The author of this book does not dispense medical advice or prescribe the use of any technique as a form of treatment for physical, emotional, or medical problems without the advice of a physician, either directly or indirectly. The intent of the author is only to offer information of a general nature to help you in your quest for emotional and spiritual well-being. In the event you use any of the information in this book for yourself, which is your constitutional right, the author and the publisher assume no responsibility for your actions.

www.teawiththemidnightmuse.com

Print information available on the last page.

ISBN: 978-1-5043-6316-7 (sc)
ISBN: 978-1-5043-6318-1 (hc)
ISBN: 978-1-5043-6317-4 (e)

Library of Congress Control Number: 2016913331

Balboa Press rev. date: 01/04/2017

Everyone has a dream to live
Everyone has a story to tell
A song to sing
A dance to dance
A poem to share
A healing journey
A medicinal remedy
A love story
A teaching to offer
A mountain to move
A gift of wild wisdom
A plan of action
A desire to express
A painting to paint
A vision to live
A legend to unfold
Everyone has a dream to live
Especially you

Your Invitation to Tea

Dear One,

If I was sitting across from you right now
drinking a cup of tea,
I would want to know
if your life turned out the way you had hoped.
I would want to know what you really want.
What has caused your heart to break?
What desire remains unfulfilled?
If you have let go of your dreams,
or if you are living them?
If you have lost hope or faith or trust?
I would want to hear about your first kiss
and the last one you had,
and how it felt and tasted.
I would want to know
if you are expressing
your deepest darkest thoughts
and your lightest loftiest visions.
I would light a candle between us,
and reach for your hand and say,
"I see you. Tell me everything."

I want to invite you to pour it all out
so that anything stuck can move
from where it has been lodged inside.
So you can make more room for
your own poetry, images
and voice to emerge.

After sufficient tears, snot
and snorting laughter,
you might ask me similar questions,
you might want to know
how I made it through and kept creating.
How I found so much aliveness,
even in the darkest hours of my life,
which weren't so very long ago.
I too had days I thought I would die.
But I didn't. And neither will you.
Conversations like this light the path.

If you asked me how I made it through,
I would tell you how writing and reading poetry
and painting with the Muse's paintbrush
gave my life to me by giving me to myself.
How I have written over one hundred poems
in the past twenty years, and created
hundreds and hundreds of paintings.
How this practice created a resiliency
which is beyond my imagination!

I would like to tell you how this was possible.
Not only possible, but joyful. Yes,
I would go so far as to say, "Creating is joyful!"
I would like to tell you,
how this being-ness called the Muse,
showed me the way into and out of the soul cave,
using language, image, symbol, hum and vibration.
How her particle and wave shaped my ideas
into matter, and how that manifestation

changed me.
How she called me forth from my tomb,
extending a red thread into the places
where I had gone dead.
She gave me words and sensations
I didn't know I even had available to me.
She woke me up and stirred my soul and
commanded me to CREATE!
And so I did.
I answered her and I created.

I would want to tell you how the muse calls
to the inherent wildness
and intrinsic goodness in me, out to play.
How she taught me about instinct
and awareness about my soul fire,
which can never ever be extinguished
and has always been burning whether
I knew it or not.
How her information connects me
to my own source. My intuition.
About how awesome access is.
How different I am because of her.
To share with you, what is possible
from being marked by her.
How she showed me where I am from.
She marks you for new life,
for a future you can call your own.
For the transforming of a life into a legend.
Then gently, but with force,
kicks your ass
until you are surely on the path,
not looking back, but forward.

Perhaps you already know her, but if not
You might ask...
How to meet this being called the Muse?
And I would say:

It is midnight and it is time
for another cup of tea
and some dark chocolate
with chili and cinnamon
by candlelight. Get your colored
markers and thick paper and let's go
on a great adventure!

Join us here in the Red Thread Café.
This is a quantum sacred space,
a place I can always go
and find her waiting for me
with a cup of tea. Ah, I see
she has placed one for you too.
Now there are three.
She called you here because
she wants to ask you unanswerable questions.
She's like that you know.
We have been waiting for you.

Welcome.
Welcome.
Welcome.

Shiloh
Sophia

Dedication

This book is dedicated to
My mama, Caron McCloud, the Poet.

She taught me to write and to draw.
She showed me how,
and most of all she showed me why.
She told me that we all
have a hidden language
that poetry and image reveal to us.

Mama only had a few rules,
and the primary one is woven into
almost every poem you will find and
every teaching held here: "Stay Conscious."
I can remember that rule from early in my life.
She felt if I stayed conscious
I could navigate the world. So far, so good.

Thank you for teaching me the Mother Tongue
of vocabulary for poets/artists:
context/content/container.
With those three I can do just about anything.
Thank you precious poet, Mama Cloud,
for the great adventure!

LOVE. TRUST. DARE. CREATE.

"We have arrived at our truths
by forgetting the parts we didn't like,
making up the parts that were missing
and holding on for dear life
to the little we came upon
that we could trust." Caron McCloud

Table of Contents

Invocations

These invocations have the power
to cast off the spells held in place
by frameworks that are not your own.
Invitations to find your own patterns
are seeded everywhere inside these pages.
The inquiries are designed to seduce
the sleeping one within you to wake in curiosity,
yawn, and stretch into soul space.
The illuminations spark insight
into the shadows of your unrevealed self.
Imagination probes that open you
to the potency of the possible are woven in.
Incantations to open the mystical pathways
that exist between the worlds.
Ideas that have been waiting for your attention.
Invitations to lick the fire
by having tea with the midnight muse.

Advance Praise Tea with the Midnight Muse

"Tea with the Midnight Muse, this book that you hold in your hands is not just a collection of poems as much as it is a treasure trove of creative reverence. A sacred portal into the living heart of divine feminine wisdom. And a soulful pilgrimage into sustainable grace fueled by wild intuitive knowing." Chris Zydel, Artist & Teacher

"Shiloh Sophia is a visionary genius. Her Intentional Creativity work, paintings, poetry, writings, and creative offerings inspire women to rise up and become who they've always wanted to be. Her writings captivate your soul and raises it up to the sunlight. If you long to feel seen and understood, look no further. Tea with the Midnight Muse is powerful medicine." Amy Ahlers, Author & Teacher

"You don't so much 'read' Tea With The Midnight Muse as 'experience' it with your whole being. If you give yourself permission to dive in to this book, candle lit, tea in hand, you will find yourself transported to a place within you that has been longing to be seen & heard. The writings bypass the rational mind and go straight to the heart of the matter. Expect to see yourself reflected in these pages, and furthermore, expect to fall madly in love with that reflection." Effy Wild, Artist & Writer

"Tea with the Midnight Muse offers are invocations to the heart and soul that can be used in your circles and classes to set a powerful field of power and possibility or that can be used for your own heart and soul, when you need to remember who you are, and that you are not alone. We often use these as openings to our circles and events". Christine Arylo, Transformational Teacher & Author

"Tea with the Midnight Muse will have you screaming YES! YES! YES!, or wiping away tears for the resonance of her words hits right to the core. It is likely she will have you questioning all that you thought you knew. Her playful and passionate expressions are filled with paradox, purpose and possibility naturally sparking a sense of wonder and curiosity." Jassy Watson, Artist & Teacher

"Shiloh Sophia sees all. Her poetry is evidence of her unabashed honesty, passion and strength. You will find a wealth of women's wisdom in her book, Tea with the Midnight Muse calls you into the reflections of your own life." Kristine Carlson, Don't Sweat the Small Stuff books

"WUNRN, The Women's United Nations Report Network, congratulates Shiloh Sophia on the publication of her book, Tea with the Midnight Muse. Over the years we have published her poetry and art on the global WUNRN ListServe, which reflects her amazing, multidimensional talents. WUNRN has found that poetry, art, photography, the creative media can be a powerful force in addressing human rights. They also balance the exceedingly serious information, documents, news, about our complex and volatile world. We have collaborated on several outstanding Panels at the United Nations Commission on the Status of Women in NYC with Shiloh Sophia where we have presented to standing-room-only audiences, programs as on Art, Poetry, and Film for Women's Resilience, Empowerment, Bonding, and for addressing Violence Against Women. Together we have shown how the cultural arts can add strength to advocacy for women's and girls' human rights, and social justice. Your poetry reaches the 'pulse points of life'..."

Lois A. Herman, Women's United Nations Report Network

UNDER THE INFLUENCE & A WARNING

Warning: Contents may have shifted during flight.

Locked doors might fly open. Hidden rooms might reveal something you didn't know existed. Strange brews might be stirred in the laboratory. The alchemists may call you to a gathering and invite you to share your medicine. You may be unexplainably called to start a large painting. You may suddenly find yourself purchasing hot pink derby hats and cowgirl boots with wings. You may fancy yourself a poet and buy a big juicy new journal. More chocolate may be consumed than usual. Your friends may start to look at you strange as a new light emanates from you. Your heart may loosen her chains. Your wounds might emit light. The cage might disappear. And why not? In the presence of the Muse. every. thing. changes.

Further, she is non-linear, a complete badass and offers very little explanation for her behavior. Don't try to get to know her, this is the wrong approach, and please, whatever you do, don't ask her where she lives or to explain her reasoning. Or she might just disappear or re-appear as the dreaded critic. One day she might be eating cupcakes in a ruffled dress and the next she may be in overalls digging bones from the graveyard of your lost self. You just never know with her.

So consider yourself warned and proceed with caution. The HOT! label has been torn from the packaging so don't be surprised if things start to burn up around here.

Muses disturb comfortable minds
and comfort disturbed minds.
Muses close old doors and open new ones.

This book is under the influence of the Muse.

This introduction is an offering to the metaphor, madness and magic of the Muse, and her place in this book. The Muse is the inspiration here, not because she is in every poem, no, she would never make herself that available – but because when I was writing these, I was with her. She was by my side, pointing to the pen and inviting me to wield it on the page.

Who is the Muse? The true answer is: I have no idea. The made up answer is that Muse is the name I call the soul self that lives within. Not exactly like the real you, but she informs the real you, and she isn't bound by the same constraints you are. Yes, muse is connected with consciousness, but more than that, she is connected with an illusive, yet ever present, wild thread that connects to your soul voice. Your inner creative life awaits you – yes, it is time to make a play date.

Muses tend to love shiny things. Not all, but many. Including poetry and painting and feather boas and red stilettos and leopard and things with wings and shimmery ribbons. Maybe that is just mine, she is rather campy and often wants hot pink neon. For you – she may ask for something else entirely when you start listening, but no matter what, know this, she is a badass and not to be trifled with. Truffled with maybe. She also likes bones, soil and salt on skin.

The Muse can be scary because you are shown things you didn't see before, or might not be ready to see. It isn't always *perty*, if you know what I mean, since we spend so much time hiding. A mystery dive into your own inner creative life is nothing to be undertaken lightly. Because things break loose from their bindings. Around here, we say, if you aren't shaking in your boots, you aren't even listening. Fear is justified. To know there is something to lose and something precious to gain makes the journey worth it.

Now this book isn't all 'about' the Muse, she emerges in a poem or two or three – but rather, these poems were written, shall we say – under the influence of the Muse. She likes to keep me up late and she picked the title, so there you have it. My hope is that the writings will awaken more of your own musings.

Consider saying "yes," and taking tea with your Muse; it's a ritual that is nurturing and inspiring. To your Muse meetings you can bring special sacred objects with you: a candle, colored pens, paper and poetry of this nature, inquiries and conversation from the in between worlds. You never know what might happen?!

Oh, and in case no one told you – your Muse can also be a dude – and the word muse is gender neutral. To meet your muse, he or she, you have to make offerings of something creative. They rarely just speak to your brain, rather, they speak in code through art, music, movement and all the senses.

How you experience access to the insights may take time to discern – but be patient – chances are your Muse has been really patient too.

As you were warned, you may fall madly in love with the universe. Or become irritated beyond measure with your current relationships or behaviors. Or wonder just what in the world you have been spending your life doing. This material isn't guaranteed to make you feel better (but it might). Rather, instead, it is here to wake you up and to shake up your ideas and reweave patterns you don't need anymore. Being unconsciously habitual can be considered a thing of the past. Poetry and art and inquiry can actually make big changes available when they weren't just moments before. Wow – what was that? Did you see that? I think it was the muse, your muse, flying close. Lean in.

Our Muse teaches us how it is possible to embrace something new and mysterious, right in the middle of our own undoing. She drops her colored ribbons to the floor in a flaming heap consuming every last unnecessary piece of unattached BS. Suddenly everything that was once held together with spit and duct tape, has come apart and lays there vulnerable in plain sight for the first time, showing itself as it burns up. POW! Now what!?

Don't blame the author or publisher if you suddenly take up the violin or begin dancing on rooftops or choose a canvas larger than your own body to paint upon. Ready anyway? Then shall we proceed? (Good) There is no going back to sleep. There is only waking into the wonder of it all. That is the best thing I can think of - falling into wonder and self discovery. Perhaps that is why this book exists. It's a love letter from me to you. A call towards something that is ready and ripe between us.

I consider it my sacred assignment to stir the cauldron of longing and chant words intended to awaken over the steaming broth that is life. There is madness in the world, precious one. Yet when we are on the path together, and creating as a tool for resiliency, we are all so much less alone. There is so much more to enjoy together as a village of awakened ones.

Our tribe, called the Cosmic Cowgirls, has been inspired by the legend that says if you are meant to meet up in this life time, then you are already connected to that person by a red thread and each thing you do is shortening the distance between you and them. Each of us has a choice of whether or not to show up for what's possible. Are you somewhere along our red thread in the distant past or future? Only you know. Perhaps you feel it in your bones.

Invocations as Creative Practices

This will give you an idea of how the book is designed and how each Invocation can become a creative practice. There are 4 parts to each reading: the invocation itself which we call A **reading**, followed by an **inquiry** inspired by the reading, then a **teaching** moment and completing it all with **imagination**.

READING: The opening Invocation is the mystical doorway of poetry. These are loosely organized in themes within chapters. Go where you are drawn; there isn't an essential order. Open and illuminate! See what arises for you from the book as if it is an oracle with its own sense of your need for that time. Read with pleasure, savored and slow, or quickly – read more than once if needed – read out loud if you choose. Then turn the page. Deep Dive!

INQUIRY: The inquiry is a probe inviting you to look at what the reading reflects for you personally. What are you seeing, feeling, hearing? What has come to mind for you? What does it make you think of, or want to create or call into being? What have you not been seeing? One might say the inquiry is how the Muse is summoned from slumber. Let her have her way with you and see what arises. The inquiry is to provoke, open, inspire, and make the material more personal to where you are.

TEACHING: A nugget of teaching expands on the reading and inquiry; widening the potential for deep seeing, translating, and putting the information to use, either through reflection or inspiration. Perhaps this has the opportunity to move the material into the sphere of transformation. Action. Has an eye been opened, a mind changed, a heart expanded? Has a hidden room thrown open the doors for you? Allow yourself to be teachable, to be changed by the simple reading of a poem on a page. In an instant we can turn experiences into transformation through choosing to be available to let the material change us.

IMAGINATION: Next you are invited to enter the sacred space of YOUR imagination through metaphor and myth. You get to go on a mini-imaginary journey to see what is revealed and to see if your Muse wants to show you something else. This is the place where you can expand even further through bringing it into your own creative zone and activating right and left brain with the heart.

Do you want to pick up a pencil and paper and draw? Do you want to write a poem, call a loved one or share a message with people you love? If you are a visual artist, are there strokes in your painting that are calling to the easel? Is there a chant or prayer being summoned?

The best way to get awesome benefit from the imagination part is to learn to let yourself see with INSIDE EYES. Meaning, just allow yourself to 'see things' instead of striving and inventing, let images and feelings arise naturally. It may take some practice and patience – but soon things will begin to emerge from your subconscious and show themselves.

The book is designed to provoke you to see yourself and the universe from a different perspective, one in which you are empowered to act, to choose, and to become, without apology, the being that you are. It is simply to become more of who you are instead of more of what the world often asks you to become. Not so easy as it turns out. This is where art and writing come in handy to provoke awareness and encourage resiliency.

That said, you can dip in at any point in which you feel called, either by choosing from the Table of Contents or just opening this book randomly. Some who have read it say they like to go in order and do one a day – others just point and shoot.

In Tea with the Midnight Muse, the reader is invited to explore the sacred, awesome interior of one's self; to reclaim one's self as relevant and vital. Sound good?

In Part One, IGNITE, the collection of poems is designed to incite and inspire your own creative inquiry process, and idea bending, as sparked by the Muse within you. These arise from writing on behalf of the Muse, and writing from a collective energy of others who may be suffering or experiencing similar challenges or epiphanies. Following each poem, if the reader wants to go deeper, there are inquiries, teachings, and imaginations. This allows you to expand upon the medicine of the poem and do your own work with journaling, insight, and drawing.

For a quick reference to broad categories you can also take a quick look at the Table of Contents and choose a topic that has the ~ ~ on either side of the word. Then read the Reading that goes with that topic and go onto the Inquiry, Teaching and Imagination.

The inquiries and teachings are kept intentionally simple, thoughts you have likely had before – but coupled with the Reading may spark insight, and action. Through inquiry – even just simple probes-the Muse begins to speak to you in new ways. Consider a new journal or mixed media sketchbook for your journey with your creative process.

Allow your imagination to run wild when you work through these, meaning, choose to see with the inside seeing eyes of the Muse. If you are invited to 'see' something or asked to feel something – tune in and do it – as so much of transformation is held within this oh so tender and simple place of inquiry. The readings, and the inquiries after are designed to create a space for YOU to have tea with YOUR Muse. Each reading can become a journal prompt or probes for poetry or sparks for drawings and muse-doodles.

These poems are good read in groups, on phone calls, in circles, workshops and to open any experience, and most of all to read with morning, or midnight tea.

We shall not cease from exploration,
and the end of all our exploring
will be to arrive where we started
and know the place for the first time.

T.S. Eliot

PART TWO: Adding Raw to my Rah Rah

Part Two, FUSE, is a personal collection, very personal, about my experiences and relationships with lovers and family, as well as some darker nights of the soul and boogy men. ACK! I took these darker poems out for about two years of the editing cycle and then brought them back in, to add gravity and shadows and raw to all my rah rah messages!

My Muse wanted some shadows in there, so there you have it. I listen to her even if it is counter intuitive.

Ring the bells that still can ring
Forget your perfect offering.
There is a crack in everything,
That's how the light gets in.
~ Leonard Cohen

Claim Your "café"

To make the experience more potent, consider you are in your own café space while you are reading. To create a context around the reading experience itself. To bring the energy and mindfulness of invocation. This is Intentional Creativity, that we approach what we are doing with reverence, intentionality and curiosity. This chosen framework prepares the mind and heart: something is about to happen: we are going into sacred liminal space.

Choosing to enter another space, yes, head and heart space, changes the brain's capacity to work with the stories coming alive on the page and in your own imagination. Our brain then can move into the potential space of the future, or full presence, instead of only referencing the past, searching for how the reading relates to us, and instead opens another world we may not have known was there.

Our community collectively calls our café the Red Thread Café which is a global circle of women who gather to share our creativity, our dreams, our prayers and work together towards the future we are inventing!

Poems with a Mind of Their Own -

These poems wanted me to tell you this. So I listened.

In one poem you may be encouraged to expand, risk and reach and in another, you may be invited to be less expanded and not have a need to perform or express. These are not contradictions of one another, but messages of expansion and contraction, like breathing. To assume that only being 'out there' and courageous is somehow good, and that being quiet and tiny is somehow not showing up, may not be useful assumptions.

This collection has made a decision to be useful. These poems want to be used, to be read at the openings of circles, at workshops, before sleep at night and upon rising, emailed to friends, and read over the phone to lovers. They want to be chanted like prayers over steaming cups of tea. They want to call your Muse from slumber and into action. They want to stir hope, inquiry, and insight. To cause a thought that hasn't been thought before to rise to the surface and change everything as you know it. Any use you have, even lighting them on fire, makes these words come alive, especially if they provoke you to write or paint!

Yes, these poems are ambitious to the point that they didn't even want to be called poems, but invocations. Poems sometimes carry their own egos. These poems want to incite action. Poems, like paintings, have a mind of their own, and often have no idea where they are going!

I wrote these rants, blessings and dares over a period of twenty years. This has been on the editing chopping block for over at least 5-6 of those, and yet, still it would need even more to be more perfect. I have long said to my students that perfection is over-rated. Perhaps revel in any found typos, it's so much funner that way. Besides, I have lost all concept of what any of this means from too many readings, and my Muse is yawning at the thought of yet another delay under the boring guise of getting it right. This material was concocted in the Muse's lab, indeed an unpredictable place existing in non-linear time.

Since I am one who chooses to be of service, I often separate my personal emotional creations from the ones I offer to the collective: ones that were inspired by the lives of those I serve and their stories. Some of these writings may or may not have been from my personal experience; they may be ones in which I was supporting someone else. Feeling into a collective suffering. I once got into an online verbal duke out with a woman who upon reading one of my writings said – why don't you just admit that's your experience? Well the truth of the matter was, that it wasn't my own, but something that was coming through – that felt needed at the time. My Muse doesn't just respond to me, she actually responds to a collective essence of suffering. A tuning in will open something that isn't in my experience but when I share it, thousands online may tell me, that was their experience. Ah, it is all mystery right? Knowing it reaches others makes it all worth while for me. I am often surprised at what I find there on the page. I ask, who is this for, and does it want to be shared? Will it help? Will it inspire? Is it needed?

As you can see, I have dedicated this entire volume to my mama, the poet Caron McCloud, for many reasons, most of all because I just want her to know how much I love her and how grateful I am for her. But beyond that, it is she who taught me how to think, to really think, and put that into words. This kind of 'thinking' has created so much freedom in my life – freedom within my being because of having access to language, and simply being aware of it and what my choices are in finding my own language. When I asked her, just before her 79th birthday, what was it that had led her to believe she could live out a life of legend, or participate consciously in the creation and experience of her own story, she replied, "I decided early on, that I mattered."

And while this volume is dedicated to my mother, I must also remember my art matriarch, Sue Hoya Sellars, who taught me that there was an inner creative life in the first place and showed me how to go there. My work of Intentional Creativity was born from her teachings to me and how to think about who I am as a creative being. And it is her question, "Who lives in here?" which has informed the ideas that shape my philosophy. My mom, Sue, and Sue's teacher, Lenore Thomas Straus are really the fore-mothers of Intentional Creativity – our creative lineage.

'Real' poets say this kind of writing (my writing) isn't 'real' poetry. Ah well I am happy to be a fake poet as long as I am a poet. 'Real' artists have also told me I am not really a painter. Thank the heavens for a spitfire magenta muse or I would have taken all this feedback to heart and stopped creating. But I didn't. Hence why I spend a lot of my life force encouraging others without 'ahem' natural talent to keep creating.

I wrote this for you. I thank you humbly in advance, for saying yes to spending some time with me in this imperfect offering. I hope you find the experience worth your while. I am ever so grateful to the women who did the read throughs of the book over the years. And to my friends, Jena, Mary, Christine, Amy and Shannon who have read/dealt with/shared this process with me in one way or another and listened to and shared many poems. And most of all, to Jonathan Lewis, my love, for making space for me to write, and to paint and for all the perfect coffee in the morning with cinnamon, cream, honey and fresh nutmeg.

I'll see you in the Red Thread Café. I'll be the one with round white sunglasses and hot pink lip gloss with my head in the stars, my cowgirl boots on the good earth and a big paintbrush in my hand. As a woman between worlds I can tell you this: Perhaps I have been looking for you and you have been looking for me.

Many of these works are gathered from a space of collective listening. Some are from my own experiences and emotions, but mostly it is something that comes through on the wings of love I have for others. This is often a difficult aspect of my work to describe but I felt I wanted to try. I listen to suffering and pattern interruption in the field and I bring my needle, red thread and if needed Grandma Eden's scissors to do the work of reweaving and mending.

You aren't alone on the quest - you will find there are others of us gathered at the Red Thread Café.

The Red Thread Café is a cosmic space in the quantum field where we meet to discuss the mysteries of the universe both in person and virtually. It's a salon, of sorts, for the Muses breaking free within each of us. So much of this is about freedom, isn't it? It is getting free of our own ideas and patterns so that something authentic can emerge from the masks we make to shield us from being seen. That's what we are up to these days. Revolution! You know, just another day at the office!

And so about 6 years after I started this book I am sending it off to the publisher. Just after my birthday #45 on the full moon in Rome. When we get home we will be working on our new live work space, a small lodge, with a classroom and my first art studio in many many years – who knows what the Muse will cook up next, her non-linear plan for my life is laughable, and yet, keeps me laughing.

Oh, and about that Red Thread, it is a sign of connection. You will see it woven throughout my work here and in legends throughout the world. It represents a quantum potential that we were supposed to connect in this lifetime, that is, if each of us shows up for the encounter.

Signed in threads, stardust and paint,

Shiloh Sophia

"The Years, of which I have spoken to you,
when I pursued the inner images,
were the most important time of my life.
Everything else is derived from this.
It began at that time,
and later details hardly matter anymore.
My entire life consisted in elaborating
what had burst forth from the
unconscious and flooded me
like an enigmatic stream
and threatened to break me."

Carl Jung, The Red Book, 1957

PART ONE

Ignite

QUEEN OF HER OWN HEART

Invocations for Self Renewal

CHAPTER 1

Dear Reader,

This collection, Queen of Her Own Heart, has to do with making a conscious choice about how you are going to show up in the world, and who you are going to become.

When we just allow the world to happen to us, we can almost experience it as an assault or onslaught, things just coming towards us of which we have no choice or control. In some cases that is so, but in others it is not. We get to be a part of what happens, and the more we practice it, the more potential we have for truly collaborating with our lives in a conscious manner.

When we decide to be at cause for our life, our many particles and how we are made up begins to change, and with that change we see what we weren't seeing before, like opportunities or relationships that reveal themselves based on how we are vibrating.

To CHOOSE to be in love with the day is indeed a choice, and one that will change our lives from the inside out. And besides, it is so much more delicious that way.

I hope you enjoy the journey here and maybe you will discover something new about the queen of your own heart and what she wants to speak to you...

Signed in the crystals from the crown of the queen,

Shiloh Sophia

After 1000 Broken Vows

After 1000 broken vows
we will rise again. I promise.
Surrendering to the mystery
of knowing and not knowing,
we finally understand
that we will not do everything
we say we will.
This confession
should feel like a relief.
We have transcended getting it right,
when we finally get it that we won't.
We can let ourselves off
our own meat hooks
when we finally know
integrity comes and goes.
Perfection is over-rated.
One fine day,
in the middle of the night,
our truths lined up single file
and went out for a midnight spree
and then didn't come home
and we woke up truth-less.
Then it is time to begin again.
Better that the heart
be broken 1000 times
than never open at all.
My job is to wipe the fevered brow
of our restless creative musings,
not demolish the hospitals

that house our sicknesses.
Though I do dream of revolution for breakfast.

This is my truth:
I have no idea what is going on.
I only know that we must create
and keep on creating no matter what.
Before the mending with red thread,
first, the breaking open.
Vow 1001 . . .
I have been waiting for you.

~ Self-Forgiveness ~

Where is self-forgiveness needed by you, for you?

We are often our own worst captor, holding ourselves caged, even when we don't need to. We set expectations for ourselves that we wouldn't expect others to keep and yet we set ourselves up to fail, based on our invented criteria. When we release our own cages, there is freedom available. Are you interested in experiencing more freedom? Imagine the cage door opening . . . creaking on the hinges and releasing. What is held inside? What did you see?

Interestingly enough, so much of living in the spaciousness of forgiveness is about choosing to allow it in, the belief that there is love available and that you can be a partaker in this love. When we move in the space of being forgiven instead of being wrong, the way we move in the world is expanded.

Let us begin with this simple clear place of inviting forgiveness. Imagine what your vow 1001 would be. What would become available to you if you released yourself? What vow? See if you can see it written in the sky, the stars, the clouds. . . .

Festival of the Open Heart

Look, there is a festival happening;
we are gathering in the streets
to be in the space of what moves us.

Stop trying to save yourself;
choose to enter into the pleasure
and chaos of being so very alive.

I know you don't feel like it;
bones, head and heart complain
and strain against the idea of this joy.

I am talking to myself here,
as artists and poets often do;
I am also talking to you.

Would we rather stay locked up
in the story of our own making
where we are always right and safe?

I don't know about you
but I am putting on my red dress,
yes, right now, and the golden boots.

I am closing the eyes that fear being seen
and opening the eyes that LOVE to be seen
while dancing in the streets of Love.

The drum that heralds the start of the festival
begins to beat – can you hear it?
Match your heart to that pace!

There are many things that would take us
away from what we love and dream of,
too busy to dance, sing, chant, pray and play.

I am not saying life isn't hard. I know it is.
I just want to choose to walk a sacred path,
instead of using all my energy in survival.

We are Divine Love on earth
and when we dance in this way
we dance with the Beloved in our arms.

To begin, we must open our arms wide enough
to let something or someone in;
let us make our way into the LOVE zone.

I will be at the festival if you want to find me.
What's that you say? Oh good. You are coming?
Because of you, this is going to be a great time!

When we are old, we won't say we regretted this.
We will say – remember the festival?
The one that changed everything?

This is, of course, the festival of the open heart.
There is a chance to join it every single day,
if we choose to take part.

I cannot think of any place I would rather be
than here with you,
moving together at the pace of beauty.

~ Living from Yes ~

How have you been withholding yourself from what you want?

Without actually meaning to, many of us have been holding ourselves back from what we really want. Whether that is from self judgment or fear, the result is we don't experience enough "Yes's" in our body and soul. We sit the dance out; we don't throw our hat into the ring; we give the seat to someone else; we just let go instead of letting ourselves have more of what would bring us delight. We let desire go dormant.

Living from the "Yes" place begins with choosing to participate, which means moving through the fear while the fear is still present. This is easier said than done; otherwise, we would have done it, right? We are afraid we will feel like a fool. Well, sometimes we will; better to embrace the fool! Will you allow less fear and more play to move through you? Just try it…

Saying yes changes how your body, mind, spirit and relationships feel, and it helps the no's- be more clear, too. Imagine you are living into your yes. See yourself as embodied as yes. What do you see or notice about you in a full body yes?

Remember You

Remember
no one can do what you do
the way you do.
Remember that what you do
is needed and wanted.

Remember
you have a unique purpose
that has always lived within you.
This purpose will continue to call on you
until you say YES!

Remember
saying YES will call upon you
to become more than you are.
This is the bliss of life,
to be the most YOU that you can be.

Remember
the key is to keep going no matter what.
You can start and stop
as many times as you need to.

Remember
unless you do this
you may always wonder, "What If?"
To try to live a dream
changes how we dream,
even if we don't reach it.

Remember
Living a dream,
is the journey, is the process,
is the dream revealing itself.
We are not waiting for a destination,
since we can live each moment truly.
Why wouldn't we?

Remember
it will sometimes seem
as if forces are against you.
When we gather up enough speed
to break through the resistances,
we often encounter obstacles.
This is not a sign to turn back.

When we move forward in our vision
energy moves towards us at that moment.
It opens up the next action,
the next door, the next opportunity.
When we take a leap of faith,
new territory opens up
that we did not see before,
and we gain access
to information not previously available.

This is glorious news!
When we risk believing in ourselves,
we will be amazed at the support that comes.
We will recognize that doing this work
is what we were born to do.

When we remember life not lived fully
is not the life we want,
then we choose.
And we choose powerfully
not to turn back again.
We may fail. We may fall.
We may even disgrace ourselves.
But what if we didn't?
Or what if we did?

Remember to remember YOU . . .
and what you are all about.
Go forward now!
And live the life you were born to live!
You belong to life
and life belongs to you.

~ Claiming Yourself ~

Have you forgotten you?

What comes up for you, when you sit with the idea that you may have forgotten parts of yourself? Isn't it odd that we think of everyone besides ourselves and sometimes wait a lifetime to go, "Hey, you know what? I have to be included here too." When we choose to make ourselves significant to the story, not only will others begin to see us that way, but our own genius will be able to make itself known. Claiming ourselves changes us (and let's the Muse emerge).

To re-member is to call back the places within you that have come apart. Remembering is a soul journey, one that causes you to go into deep inquiry if you are willing to do the work. There is some hidden sense within us that we used to be more ourselves as a child – at some other point in life, a time when our soul essence was really intact. Some say that soul is intact no matter how far you have come away from it and that when you return to it, it is as if you didn't miss a stitch! An integration begins immediately.

Imagine that you are calling these lost parts back from a vast canyon where they have been waiting. Give each part a name as they are brought home to you from a lost land, and reclaim them.

Peanut Butter for the Muse

Who is that peeking out from behind the veil?
Winking in the darkness
with the eyes you only sometimes use
She wants to know
Do you dare encounter the Muse?

A word of warning
Don't look at her with a direct gaze
She may flee from you into her own place
Leaving trails of feathers
the scent of truffles or a storm
and always the air of lady mystery

She uses your secret names to call you
as she rises to the surface of form
But where is she calling you?
To the place she dwells
You ask the address, but she refuses and sighs
Another time perhaps . . . we do have work to do

Many years could go by
before that winking blinks again
When you see her blinking
into the space between spaces
Blink Blink Blink Wink Wink
Pay attention, as the time of arrival
is near this place

Will you come this time and mystery dive?
Should you be worried, you wonder
Well, yes, she quips
You could even be scared to life instead of scared to death!

Having Muse eyes creates different lives
Don't ask what will happen or how long it will take
or if you will survive this near miss
Risk everything for this
A soul is enlightened by the Muse's kiss
If you lose her trail again,
there are things you can do to woo her,
but don't tell her I told you this:
Ask her what she likes, what she really, really likes

My Muse likes to consume my fear with
a chunky peanut butter ball
on a bit of dark chocolate
I leave it for her here
on the drawing board next to a stack of blank paper
Then I listen with the other ears within

I quiver with sudden curiosity
the blue butterflies in my belly swoop in
I pick up the pen and begin
As I hear her cry out
to the starry midnight sky:
Where oh where shall I take her?

~ Inviting Curiosity ~

Where is your curiosity taking you?

When you consider a relationship with your internal genius, your wild inner self-ness, what comes up for you? Perhaps you have heard of her counter-part, the critic, or sometimes called the voice of reason. Perhaps this curiosity can take you to meet your Muse.

Consider there is something else, another way of seeing or being you have yet to really be with and explore. What if there was so much more, more to you and to life, right here, hidden within your imagination? Will you consider it? What if this kind of thinking was the way to release your critic? As they say, curiosity kills the critic (the part you no longer need).

Imagine that within you there have been many locked doors. And that today, magically, an unseen hand begins to make rounds and unlock previously locked doors that lead to different chambers.

What do you see? What wants to be revealed? See the shapes and the colors of the doors as each one opens. You may hear locks fall to the ground with a clank. You may hear the voice of your Muse, what is her message?

Queen of Her Own Heart

Every woman is the Queen of Her Own Heart.
It isn't something she does, it is *who she is*.
She must decide how to govern her own domain.
She seeks friends and allies that honor
who she is and who she is becoming.
She has the power to create miracles.
She does not know how
or when her needs will be met,
but she trusts the will of the Divine.

Being the Queen of one's domain
is not about being
the ruler over anyone else's life or ideas.
It isn't even about calling herself a Queen.
Queenship is about self-honor.
It is about choice.
It is about knowing her limits
and setting her boundaries.
It is about learning how to live
with what comes her way
with as much grace,
majesty and justice as she can.
And sometimes, often, yes,
she has to have her own way!

She knows she has a calling to greatness within her.
She leads her own life as a grand experiment
in happiness, in creativity, and in abundance.
She offers her gifts to others,

but not to her own detriment.
She rests as she needs to,
ruling one's own life takes energy.
She chooses to embody wholeness,
her sovereign essence,
even when she feels fragmented
by all there is to do, and be.

She holds the prayers of the world within her
because she cares what happens – with everyone –
even though she cannot reach them all.
She reaches whom she can.
She often feels like she is not pulling it all off,
and sometimes she isn't.

But she keeps reaching anyway.
She keeps opening her heart
and being in her own power.
She governs her life in gratitude.
She is the Queen of Her Own Heart
She knows that
it is good to be Queen.

~ Self Empowerment ~

Are you in charge of your own domain?

A domain may be another name for the way you approach your space in the world. Many of us have been warned not to take up too much space, to keep our voices down and always be appropriate. There comes a time when we finally choose to empower ourselves, without waiting for affirmation or agreement from anyone else. How's now?

When we begin the journey towards living into self empowerment it is at first something that peaks our interest, like, "Wow, I wonder how that would feel?" as often it is a foreign experience for us to feel that. It may even feel unnatural for most of us. We can learn self empowerment, choose it and one day move into it fully.

When you have power, it isn't power over anyone but yourself and your choices. Therefore, inhabiting your empowered self doesn't require anyone else to do it for you; it is your choice.

Imagine if you considered yourself queen of your own life. What are the first actions you would take? And is there accoutrement that needs to go along with your newly dawned queenship? Something visible or invisible to others? A crown? A scepter?

Witness

Inside of you
is radiant luminous code.
Ciphers ripe for deciphering.
This seeing is what I came here for.
Some might call me an artist,
and a poet if they favor me.
I am merely a witness
to your beauty.
Inside of you stardust is begging the seams
to cross the veil of form.
Reach through and take hold of the strand
of particle and wave.
Pull it through to this place
where we hearts can witness you.
Inside of you
there is something sacred: content.
That which belongs only to you, as you.
Sometimes you don't see it, we do.
We are all witness to it.
We have need for your gifts.
Inside of you there is a great longing to be seen
but only you can fill this longing.
We already see your radiance,
yet your longing persists.
Now you know you must see yourself
to be fully seen in the way you seek.
You are your own witness.
You are the first real witness of you.
Inside of you a great call is calling

a great wheel is turning, towards you.
That which is yours to do is at the threshold,
beckoning for you to witness with your yes.
There are many ways to say yes.
Give yourself as a love offering to your own life.

~ Seeing Yourself ~

What barrier can you remove, so that you can see yourself more clearly as you are right now?

What you are is a cosmic being made of stardust. You are incarnate on this planet at this time, for a reason – can you work with this idea? You matter to the rest of us and to the world. And most of us don't know what the reason is, but in searching for it, we begin to see ourselves.

So often we have been waiting for others to see us and affirm us. This could take a lifetime of waiting. When we choose to see ourselves first, not only does it feel so much better, but it also helps others to see us. Your choosing of you as you, is not only the best thing ever, but is often the best thing for those around you too – they might not know it at first, but it is.

Imagine that you are a part of the milky way, a constellation within that luminous beauty. Imagine that you are essential to those billions of stars shining, and that you are surrounded by others also shining, a part of something wonderful - a part of creation. See yourself shimmering there in the cosmos – as if you belong. What would be different if you 'saw yourself' as wonderful. Now come back to the you that you are now – and imagine that you have brought some stardust back with you into your life. Because, you have.

Live from the Honeycomb

What if you surrender trying to be good enough
or arriving somewhere where you think you should be
or even believing in yourself in a particular way.

Sometimes these 'goal-minded' approaches
just lead you back into the same loop
you have been trying to untie since childhood.

What is needed is not to *be good enough*
or to finally believe you are ready for
whatever it is you think you should already be doing.

What is needed is *to be who you are*. Whoever that is.
To ask yourself in each moment of doubt or failure:
How can I be more me, right now?

While awaiting a nebulous breakthrough
so you can finally claim to love and believe
in yourself, there is something else . . . YOU.

To explore who you might be.
Maybe you don't know yet.
Maybe you haven't let him or her out.

Will you then, enter the honeycomb
exploring with delicious wonder
the hidden parts of your wild sweet self?

Do you dare to release the wet, wild and wise
being just beneath the protective shield
you put in place to hide you from view?

In each of the moments
when you would doubt or criticize
yourself previously, what if you stopped and asked.

The answer will always be different
than it would be if you asked:
How can I get this right, or be good enough?

This is how a life gets to be well lived
and well loved – through the journey of becoming.
Be gone silence. Be gone shame. Be gone hiding.

Trying all the time to *be good enough* or get it right
can be so boring after a while. Ho Hum.
There is something much more exciting: You.

Choose to be free enough to love what you truly love.
Savor being alive at this time in this place, *as you*.
This opens you up.

To live fully, we need to be opened.

For Valentina

~ Self Acceptance ~

How can you become more of who you already are?

When we are asking the wrong question, the answer will be wrong. The question isn't about how to be better, or more good or more perfect. It is something gorgeously different. The real question in each moment that creates different outcomes than we were getting before is, "In this moment, how can I become more and more who I really am?" This is a practice we need to remind ourselves of when we are tempted to please others, instead of be who we are.

You don't need to do anything else to become yourself except realize that is the best, and really, only place to be. We spend a lot of time putting other people on, pretending and hiding. Over time that has a real impact on our authentic voice and how we feel being in the world. Consider radical self acceptance and see what arises for you from that space.

Imagine that you are taking off garments that you no longer need. Layer by layer you are revealed. Choose three items you no longer need. See them in your visionary screen and one by one name each thing as you lay it down. Perhaps a garment of invisibility, of shame, or of blame. How does it feel after you lay them down?

Occupy Your Life

There is no place else to get to
and no other place you are supposed to be.
Honest. This is it. Really.
Your Life. Your own life.

It might not look like you thought it would.
It might not feel like you wish it did. But it is yours.
And so the question is . . .
What is stopping you from occupying it?

Why won't you pitch a tent in your heart?
Why not demand the truth
about why you aren't looking at the places
Where you are unjust to yourself?

What are you telling yourself
so you won't claim your life as it is . . . Now?
Instead of waiting for something else
better. more. brighter. to happen.

What does it mean to occupy one's life?
What does it mean to truly LIVE in one's own body?
What does it mean to LOVE
even while you are still hurting?

What does it mean to have compassion
when you yourself are feeling like a victim?
I want to know . . . what does it mean to you?
To occupy your own life?

And yes, you can choose for it to be a great one
even with how it is right now. Really.
First you ask the question: How can I occupy my life then you consider.
Be brave now in your answer, I will go first.

What it means to me is
I occupy my life.
I live like I am living
instead of living like I am dying.

What it means to me is
to keep finding the YES in every single day.
To become as present as possible,
as often as possible, and to look around.

To live the questions.
To keep my hands in creation.
To stand with my sisters and brothers
who occupy the world with chants, tears and truths.

And no matter what,
to give my great work to the world.
Whatever my great work is in each day.
To show up for it. To live it. To give it.

I want to occupy my life
as if I belong to it
and it belongs to me.
This is living.

For Mary MacDonald
aka Stella Mac

~ Embodiment ~

Will you make a choice, right now, to occupy more of your life with who you really are?

When we are living on the edges of our lives and ourselves looking in, we aren't participating in the way we could be. We are always wanting something to be better or different when the life we really need to be living is the one we have right now. Taking space is very much about the embodiment of what is, as it is, in this moment. No more waiting. We can make an agreement with ourselves not to keep playing small, and to redefine what playing big is. It is different for you than it is for others. You get to define it; that is part of occupying it, creating it according to what feels right to you. This is an invitation to move into your own skin; it is waiting for you to move in.

Choosing to occupy your life means no more excuses and a willingness to stop waiting for something else to happen.

Imagine that you are moving into yourself. See yourself as a magical alchemy takes place – you step into YOU fully. Allow yourself to feel the excitement of this choice – feel it in your body. You are just you now, with nothing else needed. How would that feel? How does that feel? Can you choose to walk around like that even for a day?

YANKING ON
YOUR CALLING
Dares for Becoming

CHAPTER 2

Dear Reader,

This collection is about personal causation: our capacity to make things happen. A moving force of self invention and personal power, and prowess! Rarrrrr! (that's a roar)

We don't know what we are capable of without exercising our muscles in the process of moving mountains, or testing our wings flying over. Who we are begins to change when we move into this life, into this body, and show up. This concept of a bucket list, or that country song 'Live Like You Were Dying,' creates a certain kind of desire to make things happen that you will have wanted to have happen before you die.

What would the list look like if you lived like you were living? The funny thing is, some of the things are the same and some are different. Living like you were living might have more to do with how you want to feel than what you need to do to be fulfilled. You could also ask your Muse what it would look like, see what she has to say. She may have different ideas about what is really important than you do.

Action is called for, greatness is invoked, and an invitation to go where you haven't gone before is available to you now. What are you waiting for? Come on. Choose.

Signed in glitter, with a bit of grit.

Shiloh Sophia

Be in Love with the Day

do you know how to be in love with the day?
really truly in love with the day?
do you know how to listen to the language of the moss
and what message she whispers to her love, the tree?
do you know how to follow the narrow trail of the deer,
to a wooded stream where God dwells?
do you know how to make kisses into medicine
for healing wounded souls?
do you know how to inhale the ocean mist
so that it makes you believe again?
do you know you are a part
of the great weave of the universe?
do you know how to hear
the raven's call to you?
do you walk down the road
you have walked all your life and find it new?
do you know how happy the daffodils are
just to be alive on that hill over there?
do you know the difference of how to love
in between the rough places and the particles of magic?
do you know how to fall in love with the day,
not just any day. this day. this very day?
this day belongs to you —
will you rise to meet it?

For Luis Martinez

~ Inviting Presence ~

Are you present?

Just tune in and see – yes or no? In this moment, yes or no, in this life yes or no? Generally – yes or no? Most of the time we walk around in a daze, not noticing the beauty available all around us, and therefore not experiencing the benefits and teachings it has for us. There is so much healing in noticing the simple beauty in our everyday experience. When we choose to tune into and fall in love with life through the senses, life falls in love with us.

It's really incredible how that works – the universe responds to us. The universe responds to our attention with giving us a greater capacity for experiencing it. To be in love with the world is to live as the mystics live, in a kind of ecstasy with the intoxication of this place. This being. Regardless of the chaos around us, this is available to us.

Imagine being in love with the day – what does your body or face look like? Feel like? How would it feel from this moment forward to say, I choose to be in love with the day? Try it! Being in love with the day opens you to the seen and unseen beauty that helps you navigate the challenges in this life. Consider taking a moment now and going towards some part of nature, outside or even an indoor plant or animal and be with it as if you being with it, changes it and you.

Just Dare

Dare to re-invent yourself
when you don't know what that looks like yet.

Dare to dream bigger than
you feel comfortable dreaming.

Dare to love unreasonably,
even if you have been hurt.

Dare to practice radical self-love
even when you aren't sure how.

Dare to practice big compassionate love
for others, even those you don't know.

Dare to say yes to your own self
when family or friends don't understand anymore.

Dare to not let fear get in your way,
and when it does, dare to keep moving.

Dare to be the most you, that you can be
while accepting yourself right as you are.

Dare to discover what beautiful means,
to you and only you.

Dare to call yourself an artist, a poet,
a dreamer, a thinker, a revolutionary.

Dare to take passionate action
so your fire will be lit within you.

Dare to take risks that make you feel hopeful
when you don't know how it will all work.

Dare be a colorful being, and to dance alone.
Dare to live. Dare to love. Dare to laugh.

Dare to not get it right. Dare to get back up.
Dare to live in amazing grace.

~ Fearlessness ~

What would you do if you knew you could not fail? What would that look like if you were being fearless?

When we can not turn back but proceed in fear, different possibilities open up for us. Our fear holds us back from what could be, because we fear what might be. A desire for security creates an illusion that can cut us off from the passion that our soul may be crying out for. When was the last time you truly dared yourself? What is your edge? What is your risky place? Look back to a time when you showed fearlessness, how did that feel?

Daring to step into ways of being we might not be ready for yet, is a risk, but when we try it on we might find joy in a new place to explore. Courage has the root of the word heart in it, from the Latin, cor, and originally had very much to do with speaking one's mind by speaking from the heart.

Imagine if you were to step out in a way that you hadn't before; just see yourself slipping through an opening that was once closed . . . where is it that you have dared to go? What is the opening like, where does it lead? What does it feel like in your body to move beyond the fear?

Yanking On Your Calling

You think answering a call is peaceful?
You think taking something from the
un-manifest to the manifest flows easily?
Ease and grace?
No.
It has never been so.
At least not as a constant.

All the moments of ease and grace
you have experienced in your life
make this moment even possible.

Callings, like birth, are messy,
bloody, hard, screaming-out-in-pain hard.

Just because it is messy, bloody, hard
doesn't mean it's bad.

Yanking something from the stardust
and shaping a golden cup of hope
is the work of warriors,
not the work of those not ready for the
long haul of manifestation.
If you don't shape the cup there will be
nowhere for the abundance
to collect in THIS realm.

Callings from the other side
need to be answered here. Yell after it.

Scream into the dark after it.
Don't let it go. Find the tail.
Pull as hard as you can until the animal
called YOUR WORK comes through a
cosmic portal onto your drawing room floor
squirming with life
begging to be expressed.

Don't listen to anything here
which doesn't serve you.

Do listen to your heart.
Do listen to your inner tugs.
Do look for the divine sparks to light up.
Do find where the pain still lives.
Do find where the light wants to shine.
Do call out to your calling
as if your life depends on it.
Because it does.

~ Manifestation ~

What are you trying to bring through into form? What does it look like, sound like, feel like?

Thinking that creating what we want is going to be easy can be a kind of self induced illusion at times! It can be easy sometimes, but other times there is a great bravery in working towards what you desire, even yanking hard because you are saying, "This matters to me. I am willing to show up and to do the work. I want it"

Many of us don't have the experience of feeling called towards something with force – it is a rather rare gift to experience a call to manifest from within one's very soul. If you do, consider yourself blessed and listen to that prompting which may have been visiting you over and over throughout your life. Would it be okay with you if there were mountains to climb to make it happen? Or you can be carried along on the river. Surrendering to the flow…

Bringing ideas into form isn't always easy. But it sure can be exhilarating. It can also be terrifying, because what if you now have to show up?! The future is uncertain for those who manifest in a dance with the mystery.

Imagine just for a moment that your calling has come into form and is there now waiting for you. Can you find any language around what it is? Can you see it? What is included in it? And what calls to you about it. Let your mind wander, and your inner eyes come to life. See what is there to be seen, don't look way – let the mystery guide your path now.

The Glitter from the Grit

May you sharpen your internal soul tools
making self excavation possible,
even, and especially, if this is messy.

May you choose to pursue your life
and your purpose fearlessly,
no matter what bills are due.

May you believe that you
don't need to be inspired to create,
and you don't need to clean the house first.

May you stop letting the inner perfectionist
make decisions that hold you back from joy,
and let expansion call you forward.

May you invite the wild self who knows
how to have a really good time
into your everyday life experience.

May you let yourself off your own hooks,
and spend more time playing hooky
and spontaneous dancing in daylight.

May you set up an art studio
in the middle of your busy full life
so self-expression transcends hobby.

May you find the tribe of folks
who are strange in the same ways you are
so you know you aren't the only odd bird.

May you believe the best about you –
YOU have something original
and unique to contribute to life.

May you listen to the compass of your own heart
and follow it, rather than the path
someone else so well-meaningly suggests.

May you meow more often, roar more often,
and be known to exclaim in a loud voice
as often as necessary what you are happy about.

May you let go of old stories that no longer serve,
and be daring and dangerous enough
to author your future.

May you move in the world
as a sacred temple of possibility,
embodying the freedom you crave.

May you have the courage
to sort the glitter from the grit of life
and revel in all the sparks of desire.

For Elizabeth
aka The Bejeweled Baroness

~ Freedom ~

What would bring more freedom to your body? Your life? Your heart?

We are the ones who impose our own limitations. By the time we are adults, no one else is holding us back anymore except our own selves. We don't even know that we are, or how we ended up that way. We are restricting the potential flow of freedom available to us. We don't need to.

A sorting process may be needed, a separation from the behaviors that have kept us trapped from the behaviors that liberate. It doesn't happen overnight, but day by day, relationship by relationship, we examine what feels good and what doesn't. Often what feels good creates and allows for freedom. What doesn't, constricts. Begin with noticing where the constriction is and gently releasing. . . .

Imagine you are looking at a pile of rubble, could even be compost, but that you are looking for something precious. Be willing to dig, and to watch for that which rises to the surface. Don't let the muck get in the way, just search and find. Being a self searcher is a kind of freedom most people don't even know about. What did you find? Use your imagination to SEE the pile itself.

From there imagine that you have claimed freedom from the pile – that you no longer need to be held back by the pile, or the past – or anything. See if you can find and nurture that freedom in your own body and spirit. External circumstances don't need to change – just the internal ones. That inner change is what provides a new view.

Finding Wings

The act of finding wings is
a life long journey in and of itself.
We cannot wait for inspiration to strike
or circumstances to improve.
The time to take wing is always
and ever right now.
Right now.
Right now.
and
Now.
We each have to find
our own wing cadence –
the pattern within
an invisible force
right at our back,
on each side of our arms
waiting to fill out and lift us.
We can practice knowing
the force of life is there.
We can pretend we feel it
even when we don't.
Especially when we don't.
Imagine the whole
gorgeous universe
has your back.
You don't have to
rely on your strength only.
Imagine that preening your feathers
is vital, important work.

Expecting miracles
is your spiritual practice.
Lift your wings.
Feel their power lifting you.
Flap, flap, flap,
hear the sound . . .
Now, look
what is it you are flying toward?
What comes first?
The dream or the wing?

~ Support ~

Do you allow yourself to feel supported by the universe?

Sometimes what is needed is to just begin to make subtle movements forward. A kind of remembering into what's possible that you may have forgotten or temporarily put aside.

There is this amazing support from the universe available all the time to those who are willing to change, dare, and open to it. Those who exhibit bravery in stretching even in small strides will often feel a lift, an unseen hand guiding, perhaps even the strength of their own wings developing power. It doesn't always feel this way of course, feeling supported is a kind of practice in and of itself. Are there areas where there could be support but you are withholding yourself from receiving it?

Imagine what it would feel like for you to allow yourself to just feel supported right now, to just practice moving out of the 'all alone' story, and move into being supported, even without evidence to encourage you. Just through choosing it.

Imagine that this is normal instead of the exception. What energy is different when you come from the space of having what you need to go where you need to go and do what you need to do? What happens if you just say − I am supported?

See an image of yourself being surrounded by support − what do you see? Is there a symbol, color or pattern, or even a sensation that represents this feeling for you? Hold onto it dear one, this is an important space for you − for all of us.

This is No Ordinary Day

This is no ordinary day.
But then, none of them are.
I mean…
What if you are not who you think you are?
What if who you really are
hasn't even happened yet?
What does it feel like
to consider that your whole life
may well be in front of you
instead of behind you?

There are places between places
where the true mind
and the true heart connect.
This is the only place
from which to make choices.

Open your closed off places,
even if it hurts.
Pull off the scabs today.
Yes, right now.

There is an up-swell inside you.
You were given no language for it.
It is that which now begs to be said.

Do you know what it is?
Are you willing to look?
To listen? To feel?

Or will you stay there where you are,
gazing out the window of the past
wondering where all the good days have gone?

The up-swell you feel
is the gift in you waiting
to be born again.
Waiting to rush
onto the pages of your life and
consume every mediocre thing
in its path.

Do you think it wise to wait?
Wise to count the cost until
the opportunity passes?

The up-swell won't make
logical sense on paper.
It won't want you
to tell your friends what you are up to.
But I tell you this,
if it is the last thing I ever tell you . . .

Follow the up-swell of your emotional heart
where it leads you. Yes, of course
you will be hurt. But you will be hurt
regardless. Didn't anyone tell you?
This is a part of becoming more human.

~ Self Inquiry ~

What if you aren't who you think you are?

Inquiries like this can sometimes be a part of waking us up. Sometimes we have settled into a self with default settings that might not really be who we are. We can be so busy covering up, passing, and acting a part – that we don't realize we have become something or someone else. This actually happens all the time, for some it may arise as an identity crisis.

Are you open to seeing and knowing and feeling something that you haven't experienced before? This is a choice to explore a new framework that begins with inquiry – frames of possibility may open up before your eyes, this is what we hope – that you will see that who you are is still unfurling. Life isn't just happening – to you – you are happening to life.

Imagine that you can see a golden thread in the shape of a tree, it's etheric yet tangible. See it moving from your heart to your mind and blossoming out. See the connections and the light moving along the threads back and forth creating a reciprocity of light. Be interested in this tree of light – look at it as if it is you. What do you see? Now ask yourself a few questions about you. This might not be easy – but try it – consider – what do I really want now? What does my Muse want to show me? What is calling me now?

She Surrenders to Change

she surrenders to change
she dances, chants, prays, seeks
she does what she knows to do
to bring healing to her temple body
to bring clarity to her sound mind

to bring joy to her soul
to awaken her heart to love's fire
to honor her relationships
to nurture her spirit
she moves beyond her limitations

she dares to create
she connects to her truth
she forgives what she can
she accepts what she must
she gives up shame

she reaches out, she reaches in
sometimes it feels like it isn't working
she falls down and cries and listens
she breathes, moves on
she rests when she needs to

she sets new boundaries
she releases old rules
she invites new experiences
she tends her garden
sometimes she feels it is working

she leaps and shouts and
grows new little sprouts
she is abundance, she is a tree of life
to those that embrace her
she evolves, she shines

she falls in love with herself
she is transforming
of that, she is sure
she celebrates her journey
she says yes to miracles

she heals and moves on
she embodies her gratitude
and offers it on the altar of earth
she grows orchards of fruit
in her flowering soul

~ Allowing ~

Where do you need to give yourself a permission slip?

We are all hard on ourselves. It's strange how natural it is to be critical of our tender selves. But we often just are, until we learn another way of being. Learning another way might take practice, maybe even spiritual practice, that includes things like prayer or dance or chanting or writing or being in nature or writing or reading poetry or asking yourself questions like this.

When we allow change to move through us without too much resistance – then striving can decrease. We can allow the spaciousness of what wants to happen, happen, and move. We are very good at being busy making things happen, and not as good at allowing things to happen through us and to us in their own natural timing. There may indeed be a divine timing, and since we don't really know – why not give it a try?

Allowing takes stepping back from causing, and seeing what wants to be revealed. Are you ready to create more spaciousness for yourself? From that place, Imagine you are giving yourself a permission slip – what color is your permission slip and what does it say? Read it out loud or write it down. Maybe hand a few out to people you know.

The Healing Fields

how does healing happen?

is it . . . forgetting a little at a time
that which hurts and waking up one morning
just feeling a little bit lighter?

is it . . . finally forgiving yourself and the world
by understanding, somehow,
we are all wounded with you?

is it . . . realizing the world is whole, after all,
or accepting that the world is broken open
and has need of your love?

is it . . . noticing a whole day, week or month has gone
by without beating yourself up in the old ways that have
held you back?

is it . . . being struck by a compassion so tender
you know it must belong to the Beloved
since you don't recognize this kindness in you?

is it . . . realizing this is just how it is right now
and somehow it is oddly, unreasonably,
not personal or about you at all?

this is our human story that we are creating together.
can we get 'free enough' to create in it,
with true personal intention?

is it . . . not letting your wounded songs hold you back
from that which sings to you
within your deepest soul cave?

is it . . . allowing shadow-work and light-work
to co-exist without striving for either one to be greater
or better or good or bad?

is it . . . being willing to lean into your resistances until
the edge of your hardened places creates
tender spaces?

is it . . . being willing to surrender your cynicism and
complacency even when you know the ridiculousness
of the harm going on?

is it . . . opening your heart, yes again and wider still,
to a new face, a new heart, yes, a new chance even in
the same old life?

is it . . . letting go of making the hard things
into stories of meaning about why it went down this
way or that, what if there is no real reason?

is it . . . surrendering enough to allow old patterns
to dissolve, even when they have served you so very
well, or so you thought?

what if nothing is as you thought it would be
or have believed? it might be something even better,
I don't know, but maybe . . .

each one of these stories we have talked about
are 'fields' of energy living within us,
weaving our luminous patterns to life.

lay down the burden of what you thought
you knew and just come
and open with us to your part in the unfolding mystery.

when you are too laden with all the past stories
and it is too crowded to gather your harvest
let's make space to expand.

don't worry, everything has become compost and is
useful – these old stories become legend in no time,
we will be amazed what good can come from them.

everything happens in cycles,
this may have been a longer one
than you felt you could survive, but you did!

I have come for you, take my hand now and rise up
the others are waiting for us
to take our place in the circle.

I have no idea what will happen
but I imagine it will be
better than you think.

your harvest is happening now, even if you don't see it,
just come, we have been calling your name.
you'll see

this kind of healing looks different than we thought
we had hoped for a total recovery
and peace on earth.

instead we have been sent
to learn each other's stories whole, the healed story
begins with this dance, yes, this one.

we will start this dance with giving thanks
for the bounty and raising our hands in praise
for the life-giving Beloved.

we have arrived in the healing fields
and we will nourish and be nourished here
where generosity is freely given and received.

For Misty Frederick Ritz and Tina Greene

~ Seeking Healing ~

What healing is it that you currently seek?

Has there been a healing that has eluded you? Once you have considered what healing you are seeking and or grappling with, as is sometimes the case, you are invited to just sit with it gently, like holding it as a feather in your hands. What color is the feather? How light is it? Do you feel it touching your fingers?

Then ask yourself, "Is there a story I have been telling myself about this particular healing? What is the story?" Often with healings there is a time to get conscious with what we have woven around it and what we have made it mean. This doesn't make it go away – that would be nice, wouldn't it, if once we got to the root of it, it actually changed? But no. Getting conscious is an early stage of healing.

Imagine that the healing you seek is that feather. Consider infusing your healing intention into this feather. Then with open hands gently put it down, saying, "I am right here if you need me, but I won't grasp for you or try to lift you up. A wind could carry you off if you like."

And then look towards something new that would be possible if this healing was indeed underway. It won't be rushed, but it may allow itself to take up less space. Simply by your tenderness, the grip of it can be less. Just notice if it already feels lighter. Imagine the feather floating off on a gentle wind.

LIVE LIKE YOU ARE LIVING

A Call to Show Up

CHAPTER 3

Dear Reader,

I love to live life as if it is a continual invitation to join it right where it is. As if there is a constant happening, happening and I get to include myself in that. To choose it.

Many of us spend, or even waste, a lot of time 'sitting this dance out'. Waiting to be asked, picked, chosen, claimed. I see a lot of suffering around this idea of wanting to be found. My call here is to claim yourself, include yourself, stop waiting, be counted. This isn't second nature to us — so it is hardly ever easy.

I would go as far as to say that not choosing ourselves soon enough leads to relationships where we continue to need something we are rarely going to get. It also puts the focus outward, on the world or on those who propose to love us, to make us feel special and wanted. And while I don't know anyone who doesn't want to feel wanted, and that is so totally how most of us feel — I do know there is another way that can work wonders"I'm in" or "I'm ready" or, I am showing up no matter what. Here I am.

As you read through this collection, starting with She Danced, a very early work of mine, may you consider including yourself in a way you haven't before. Consider this your invitation. It is you know, this IS your invitation.

Signed with a starry tip of a dancing cowgirl boot in the dirt,

Shiloh Sophia

She Danced

she danced for the love she felt
the love she gave away
and the love she kept

she danced to free her spirit
and to free other spirits too
she danced in response to joy
and to process pain
she moved her body
like her life depended on it
praying for love to come
for sadness to go

she danced for all the people
who can't dance for themselves
she also taught others to dance
for justice, for truth, for possibility
for healing the broken-hearted
she danced to break the ties that bind
our women ~ our mothers ~
to bring awareness and healing

she danced to break open the hearts of
our men ~ our fathers ~
to bring truth and compassion
to invite friendship and art
into the open spaces
that the dance created
she danced
to keep the flame of true love burning
she danced when she was too tired to walk
she danced between the worlds

she danced because a celebration
calls for dancing
the twirl of skirts, the rhythm of feet
the snapping and clapping
the exultant inhale and exhale

she danced with lovers, she danced with friends
she danced alone too because some nights
we all dance alone and because sometimes
dancing is all that can be done

she danced for the artists and musicians
and scientists and alchemists and midwives
and physicians and housewives and gas stationers
and waitresses and for all who work
too too hard, for too too little

she danced for all the creators of invention
and those whose gift is just TO BE
she danced to dislodge the caught gifts
struggling to get free in each of us

she danced for the living and for the dead
in birth and in mourning
for peace, beauty and creative expression
she danced our prayers all the way to GOD
which isn't so very far after all . . .

"Shall we dance?" asked the Creator of Dance
they danced until the sun came up
and this time she didn't have to lead

For Shannon Cinnamon McCloud

~ Compassion ~

What burdens do you carry for the world?

There is a lot of crazy stuff going on all the time in our lives and in our world. And then there is the particular unique burden or presence in our hearts that we are dealing or grappling with something or some kind of care that weighs on us about the suffering of others. It is specific to each person, and when articulated may not sound as a significant call to someone else's ears. But to you it's important. Each of us must identify the thing that weighs on us and move into it through art, dance, song, and other catalytic experience. We call this intentional creativity – to create with intention around a particular thing.

That is the way that a burden can be moved into the spaciousness of compassion. Compassion cannot be invented; it has to be felt as truth in your heart. And it won't come before you are ready. When you can learn to dance with the heaviness you carry, then there can be movement. That movement might be just enough for you to see it – you don't have to carry it yourself to love it and have true compassion for it.

Imagine that you are dancing with the Divine. Can you see your head tilting back as you are carried along the places where you don't know the way or when are tired? Feel yourself being held and guided. Let yourself dance in the freedom of knowing that the dance will take you to the next place you need to be. That you don't have to save everyone, you just show up for the dance.

To Be Glorious

Today, I choose myself.
I choose to be the Queen of my own domain.
To name myself as the one who governs my life.
Today I choose loving myself.

I shall not wait for the approval of others.
I will act on my own behalf and inner knowing.
I choose to listen to this great heart within me,
to honor what it wants, needs and longs for.

I shall no longer allow the sacred parts of myself
to feel worthless, fragmented and isolated.
I choose to take up space in this Universe.
To inhabit this vessel of self, which is my holy temple.

I shall not keep my gifts hidden any longer
or allow fear to keep me from my greatness.
I choose to be as wonderful as I truly am.
To explore just who I might be, after all these years.

I shall not judge myself for where I have not
journeyed yet, or the ways I have been untrue.
I choose to forgive myself and release the old stories
to make space, legends even, to emerge.

I shall not forsake my dreaming
or allow others ideas to crowd my own.
I will think my own thoughts.
I choose to fall in love with who I am, as I am.

I choose to embrace the messy
and the marvelous within me.
I shall not diminish my light.
I shall shine.

I choose to see myself as whole, worthy, wildly me.
I choose to be so much more than enough.
I choose to be outrageously, fearlessly embodied.
Will you join me in this freedom?

Being glorious is not a default. It is a choice.
Today, I choose myself.
I choose to be glorious.
Will you join me here in this beauty?

Hear me now. I choose to see myself,
and to be seen by you, too.
And to see you, too.
See me . . . seeing you . . . yes . . . right now.

For Christine Arylo

~ Self Love ~

What would it be like to be in love with who you are, as you are?

Choosing oneself isn't something we are taught, or even something that comes naturally. It isn't something we came in with; it is something we have to learn, often because we have fallen out of sync with our natural state of potential being.

Our issues of unworthiness often come into our lives due to how we are treated by others, and eventually how we treat ourselves. One day we wake up and realize the way we have been viewing ourselves is out of control! Maybe shame, self-hatred, and body hate have even became our primary view of ourselves! When it is time to change, we will gradually begin to transition to this other more glorious potential of loving ourselves, simply because we know it exists.

Imagine holding yourself to your heart with utter tenderness. You may even feel a desire to apologize. Tell yourself your are sorry for the ways you have been unkind. Take the time you need. Then make a new vow to explore the choice to love yourself. It might not happen overnight – that isn't what matters, what matters is that it begins, and it begins, now. What is your new vow. Maybe share it with someone or write it on a mirror in sharpie. Post a selfie with the words, make it real.

Bountiful is a Way of Being

Bountiful is a way of being.
Bountiful is something we choose.
Bountiful is a place within
which we cultivate over time.

We cannot always choose our circumstances.
And we cannot always choose
our responses in the moment,
as hard as we may try.

Bountiful is something that comes
after things have been hard
and doors have closed.
It is what we do with what we have.

It is how we create who we can be in the world.
It is a decision to be a blessing,
to create a different frame of reference,
one that is in our own favor.

If we just evaluate what we have and possess,
who we have been up 'till now and
measure it against the world measuring stick,
we may not feel bountiful at all.

We may even feel downright discouraged.
This is why we have to choose
to be bountiful, no matter what.
This takes courage.

We get to choose creativity
and the peace that passes understanding.
This is a gift from the Creator,
to be able to find bliss in chaos.

Bountiful is a spiritual practice,
a love ritual, a peace offering,
a powerful tool for healing,
a rite of passage.

For Dori Etter

~ Being Bountiful ~

Where can you bring an experience of bountifulness to your life?

Are there places that feel scarce or frail or thin? What would it be like to bring an expression of bounty there? Scarcity is usually a default setting when things don't turn out the way we hope or dreamed. And we are often told we get to have our dreams if we want, but we don't always, and then we are disappointed. We may turn to, "Why me?" or "What's happening?" or "What did I do to deserve this?" These are the kinds of thoughts we have when we aren't mindful about change, because abundance is an ebb and flow, and it is natural for it to contract and expand. Bounty is an expansion and contraction, but we usually only relate to the expansion, as if that is where it's at. There is also something about the emptiness, or the rest or the void, or the mystery - if we can sit with it, and then choosing again to be bountiful when the natural rise comes again. Our bounty should not be based on what we have, but the way we view ourselves and how we engage with life.

Imagine that bounty, like a scattering of gold stars, is spread out before you. So generous you don't need to do anyting but enjoy it. It isn't there because you deserve anything; it's just there because of grace. What if these gold stars were just grace. A gift. Where in your life is this already happening? Also consider that to be bountiful, being generous is a big part of the process - is there somewhere you need to practice generosity? The spirit of generosity is the hidden path to being bountiful.

Fear Less, Love More

fear less
love more
doubt less
dream more
mock less
hope more
sleep less
create more
plan less
express more
judge less
laugh more
gossip less
listen more
spend less
make more
control less
surrender more
distract less
kiss more
hesitate less
dance more
pretend less
be more you
think less
receive more

~ Being More ~

Where would you like to take up more space? Have you ever had someone tell you that you are just too much or too big for your britches? Simmer down. Who you do think you are? MOST of us hear these messages as young children and without realizing it we begin to hem ourselves in, and to monitor our self expression. We do it out of self preservation; the only thing is that once we are adults and we can make choices for ourselves, we usually don't! We may need to keep being reminded. Consider this a reminder! We can spend years trying to fit in and the trouble is, if we aren't being who we are then we are likely trying to fit ourselves into the wrong fit anyway. Are there ways you have been hiding from your bigness or compensating for your smallness? If so, is there something that is calling out to you right now that wants to just expand?

Imagine something in your life you have kept small growing gently into its natural form, neither bigger nor smaller than it needs to be or should be, just it's natural size. See it in your minds eye – hold it there as a symbol of personal, brave expansion, a place where you are in charge and no one can tell you that you are taking up too much space. Do any images emerge? Symbols, patterns, designs.

This is your time. It has always been yours. We are just often surrounded by others who tell us it isn't.

I don't want to impress you

I don't want to impress you.
I refuse to perform to make you love me.
Looking good is exhausting.
Especially if you have to keep it up.
Being right is so last life time.
I am not invested in hiding to protect myself.
This doesn't mean I am surrendering.
This means my soul has plans for me.

I just want to be as I am called to be.
I am spontaneous, a badass, unpredictable at best,
and if you still love me, awesome. I love you too.
I would much prefer to play together
than look good by myself.
I don't care about being right,
I would rather just be with you. Okay?
This doesn't mean I am surrendering.
This means my soul has plans for me.

You know this already,
to be yourself takes crazy courage.
The kind most of us are born with.
But somehow, we tuck it away to protect others.
Or, even worse, we forget.
People can be afraid of people like us,
and try to shut us down,
it isn't too hard, since we don't want to offend.
That doesn't mean I am surrendering.
This means my soul has plans for me.

When we are too shiny, we scare people.
That's okay. Tell them what all the sparkle is about.
Tell them your shine has spilled out,
that the edges of your container have expanded.
Invite them to dance in the scattered radiance.
Tell them not to surrender to the way things are.
Tell them, their soul has plans for them.

~ Return to Authenticity ~

Where are you being the least authentic as it relates to how you show up in the lives of others?

Do you feel like you have to stop being who you are in order to 'fit in' or be appropriate? Sometimes we do this to pass or to not stand out. Yet we do it so long we forget the parts of ourselves we were hiding and may not easily locate them again. Sometimes the parts we hide are the most creative, wild and free...the price of letting those go is significant over time. We become "conditioned" to hide.

The weird thing is we do it long after we don't need to or with people we don't need to – it becomes the new normal. For some of us – bringing those lost parts out can feel like work and or as if it will put us in jeopardy. The cost to our own authenticity is tremendous.

Imagine that you are fully integrated – having called back the lost parts of you; and you are standing in your own authenticity. Allow yourself to feel the fullness, the wholeness. See yourself as fully intact. Ask that image of wholeness that you see - to show you yourself, being as authentic as you possibly can? What do you see? And is there an action you can take to bring that authenticity into expression – today?

A Regular Person

What if I am just a regular person?
And I don't want to soar and strive.
Everyone keeps saying GO GO GO
and my heart and mind keep saying
NO NO NO. You're okay as you are.

Maybe I am content with the day to day.
What if creating goals beyond my reach
makes me feel inadequate.
What if saying 'I love you' to myself in the mirror
feels irrelevant – You mean, I don't?
I didn't know that until you told me.

What if I don't have a great need to fill for myself
or a need to fulfill for the world?
Does that make me a bad person?
Does everyone need to be great?
Maybe the not-so-great people
make the world go round.
Perhaps all the cheerleaders
who say BE all you can be
need to stop trying so hard to convince me.

I alternate between feeling connected and not,
but that seems pretty normal to me.
Why is everyone trying to sell everyone else
on being better all the time?
Who made up these rules?
Maybe they are trying to sell me something
I don't need, and if I listen, I will think I do.
I don't mind you if you need it
as long as you don't mind if I don't.

~ Just Being ~

Where do you feel you are being pressured to be something or someone you are not?

Are there places and spaces in your being where you feel squished or contorted or expected to be like someone else? This can also cause there to be feelings of inadequacy that come out of the blue and bonk you on the head. Is there a freedom that comes into view if you aren't trying to be better all the time and can find some simple contentment with who you already are?

What would it be like to just be, and not have to be all you can be? What comes up for you when you think of that? It may be counterintuitive because even the most well meaning parents and teachers have told us we can have it all if we work hard. Lots of stories out there that might not be our ours at all.

Imagine that you are laying down all the burdens of pressure. One by one you just set them down, not unceremoniously, but as if you just don't need them anymore. You may spell them out or write them out or speak them out. Allow yourself to feel lighter in the potential state of just being regular, even normal. Is the pressure easing up? Allow it to feel different in this moment, a release is here for you.

Not Enough

You think you are not enough
and so that means what you do
is never enough.
I think the story
"I am not enough"
is a lie.

I am wondering
why we –
intelligent, lovely, brave
souls that we are –
would go on believing a lie?

Today is for shedding old stories
and I am wondering
who is ready to shed that one?
Or another one
that is no longer needed?

Ready. Set. Go.

When you are done
you can join me right here.
The truth is:
we are more wonderful
than we can imagine
and it is a miracle you were born.

We have lived long enough
thinking "not enough"
is a way of being. It's not.
Why not invent a story, about who you are?
One you would just LOVE to tell.

For Amy Ahlers

~ Being Enough ~

Where have you been being too hard on yourself?

Are you ready to surrender the "not enough" lie? It's a famous one and most of us deal with it at one point or another. In fact, it almost stalks us. We get reminders to be more than we are, all the time, which creates less than. What about just right, just enough, and furthermore, according to who? Who is defining our enough-ness?

If it is time you defined your own enough-ness then why don't you just say it? That you are done with being too hard on you. Making us think we need more to be complete is part of the messed up system to make us buy stuff we don't need, to fill a hole they told us we have, but we don't. At least we don't have to have it. Imagine that. Want to join the rest of us who are choosing to be enough? It's way better over here. There are more and more of us, and we can certainly relate to the experience of never being enough.

Imagine that there is nothing else you need to do or be or say or create – that you are ALL RIGHT just where you are without one more thing needing to change. Just for the moment, or an hour or a day, explore a new truth, one where you are enough as you are. If you see yourself as ENOUGH, is there a symbol that represents that for you.

To Be Wonderful

I have heard
there are some
who do not condone
others being wonderful.

I have heard
some do not want
others to shine.
Don't listen to the light-dimmers.

Beware of those
who think being small
is somehow being appropriate.
It is not always appropriate to be appropriate.

Have you ever felt not quite yourself around some folks?
Do you ever feel like you being a success,
or just being happy,
appears to be threatening to others?
Even those who love you (and they really do!).
I have even heard the words,
"healthy competition,"
to explain meanness or pettiness amongst us.
I think it is only when we feel small ourselves
that we have a need to make others feel not so tall.
What if we sought to lift one another up?
Our shining invites others to shine.

I am not speaking of pride, or self-importance.
I am speaking about living a life where
being wonderful is encouraged.
Supported. Called forth. Invited.

What if you could be as wonderful
as you feel like being?
Be as big as you want to be,
be as bright as a shining star?

What if you did not have to apologize
for being blessed?
That would feel good.
Just to be blessed and be in blessing.

The Holy One of All Creation
has endowed us each
with unimaginable beauty of one kind or another.
We cannot allow others to tell us it isn't so.

Even if things are good with you,
they may not be okay with your neighbor,
and so being wonderful might seem, well . . .
Outrageous. Audacious. Fearless.

And it is. But I say you can be wonderful.
You can have ecstatic, wonder-filled moments,
or hours, or days or a whole lifetime.
Go for it! Do it! For all of our sakes.

To be wonderful is a combination
of choosing to let your light shine
and receiving the love that is yours.
Nurturing the light in the cycle of waxing and waning.

Not everyone will see your light or acknowledge it.
The Holy One sees it. And you can see it.
For what it is worth,
I see you and I think you are Wonderful.

For Michelle Fairchild

~ Shining ~

Are you willing to let yourself shine?

What would shining look like for you? You get to choose the wattage and voltage and when and how you glow. It isn't something you are just born with and then that's it – you can increase it through focusing on it – isn't that cool? We get to raise our own lights and in tandem, others lights are raised around us.

Isn't it strange how many people seem to be wanting to keep us down, until we realize what's happening and begin to rebel against this competition thing, which is all invented anyway. Shining is something that comes naturally when we are given an environment in which shining is encouraged! But how many of us get to hang out in those places? Let's create them ourselves.

We have to search for the other hidden shining ones who are also wanting to shine, not wanting to dim others' lights to increase their own, and invite them to tea with us. We can remind each other about our lights and practice ways of being that encourage being bright instead of dimming down - in order to not offend or fit in. Have you been told not to outshine someone, often a schoolmate or sibling or friend? Sometimes this goes right into our heart and that very day we stop or diminish the glow. We didn't know better, but now we do. We have other choices.

Imagine that you are full of light, just glowing from inside – pink, yellow, white, gold sparkles shimmering – and let it start inside and begin to just move outward and around you until you are surrounded by your own unapologetic light.

FIRE OF THE SPIRIT
Sparks to Light the Path

CHAPTER 4

Dear Reader,

A volume of poetry would not be complete for me without working with the concepts of the Sacred and the Feminine. For me, this is a relationship with the one I call the Great Lady. Yes the Blessed Mother! Or as some call her, the BVM. You will see reference to Her in much of my work, paintings and writings.

My spiritual path is very connected with the nature of the Universe, nature itself, and geeky science! I love the idea of bio-photons, of the light that emits from us, being able to be amplified through love and shared with others. So cool. Through our intention and conscious awareness we can literally LIGHT ourselves up and send our love to others. For me this is evidence of what's possible in the spiritual and quantum realm that we cannot see with the eye, but can feel in the heart and body. We are always saying we are 'sending our love' but perhaps we didn't know how very real that was.

I am in love with the idea that the spark that is within us was a spark off of the ole' fire of Creator. And that at my conception I was a traveling spark from the Creator's heart that lighted upon the potential egg I hatched out of. When I write, it often feels like prayers and blessings, a holy time. I feel a sense of connection with the sacred. I feel like I am writing to someone, to you, to a cosmic someone on the other end of my red thread. Thanks for being here in the temple of creativity with me.

Signed in a scarlet thread from the hem of her garment,

Shiloh Sophia

A Prayer to Great Spirit

Great Spirit of Life
I offer myself to You this day.
I invite Your will and Your way
to flow as living water in my life.

I acknowledge the power of goodness
is the force in my body, spirit and soul.
I ask for protection
and guidance.

I ask every cell and system
to listen to this prayer for healing.
I celebrate and honor the intelligence
at work throughout my body.

I celebrate and honor the love
opening my heart in this moment.
I invoke my inner wisdom
and understanding.

I believe healing is possible
and right now in this moment,
healing is mine.
I receive this wholeness.

I trust the mystery of the great unknown
works in ways I cannot see or know.
This prayer for transformation frees my energy.
I choose to feel more free right now!

I am willing to do the personal work needed
to sustain my own healing journey.
This moment I practice the feeling of wellness,
I practice my spiritual path with intention.

I do not allow guilt and shame to live in me.
I forgive myself and those I can forgive, I do.
I call forth the power given me to heal
by the Great Spirit of Life, and I give thanks.

I send a prayer of healing to those I know,
those I am yet to know and those I may never know.
May we all experience healing and transformation,
in as much as we are able to receive it.

May the waters of life flow through my body.
May the fire of passion purify my heart.
May the sweetness of earth enrich my soul.
May the tree of life bless my creativity.

May the breath of the Divine awaken my mind.
May the Great Spirit embrace my great spirit.
My faith is making this healing possible.
May it be so, and so it is!

Amen

~ Tending Fragile Faith ~

Where do you feel your faith has become fragile?

Faith can be tricky because it means different things to different people. And it is one of those words that can make you wonder, "Do I even have it?" And if so, is it based on things going right? When things go wrong do I then doubt the faith I had?

Ponder for yourself where you reside with your faith story – do you have one? How would you describe it? Are there new places that want to show themselves to you simply because you are showing up to ask the question? Faith is something we can choose to make ourselves available to no matter what is going on in our lives . . . not the faith that says it is going to go my way, but the faith that says when it doesn't I will go ahead and trust anyone. We don't get to know the mind of the Divine, or choose how this goes. But we get to choose how we show up in it. We get to choose to surrender to now, knowing and finding a way to trust anyway. It is indeed a mystery.

Imagine that you did have faith in the great unfolding, that you may not know how, but that somehow there is a trust in what's happening. How would that be different than where you are now? See yourself being in alignment with a spiritual path. See yourself walking along that path. What do you notice about the path? About you on the path? Is there anything you can see or sense?

Fire of the Spirit

May the Fire of the Spirit
spark us when we feel despair.
May Her Holy, glistening flame
catch our breath,
wake us up,
get us moving.

May the Fire of the Spirit
stir our hearts when we feel alone.
May Her radiant presence inspire us
reaching out and reaching in
so we do not stay in hard places too long.

May the Fire of the Spirit
burn through self-pity.
May Her cleansing power
shed the layers,
scrub the old skins to the floor
so we might begin once more.

May the Fire of the Spirit
encourage us to create.
May Her bountiful wisdom
spark our creations
and may we in turn, encourage others
and light up the world with our love.

For Ama Zenya

~ Light in the Dark ~

What area of your heart needs to be lit up right now?

Is there a place that feels neglected or dark that could use some loving energy? Would you be open to, in this moment, allowing love to come into those places as it was really happening (because it is)?

Allowing the love to come is a huge part of what lets it come in. Seems simple, right? But we know it isn't. We are often attached to what we have been wrestling with, even if we don't know we are. What if part of the solution was just saying Yes to letting it come in? Making ourselves available to feeling just a tiny bit better?

Imagine that there is love light pouring through the air towards you right now. See it shining on the dark places that need light and air. Allow it in and if really brave, even smile, as it helps the light get through. What colors do you see? Pretend you can see the light itself (it is there even if you cannot see it). Then, there is this funny thing about light, if you share it, it expands. Is there someone you want to share your light with?

Our Lady of Everything

our lady of everything
precious mother
hail, ma abundant
so full of grace
blessed art thou
among all beings
we who know you
beyond titles and concepts
blessed is the life-giving fruit
of your tree of life womb
wholly mary-ma
mother of god
praise you
for praying for us
now and in every hour of our need
you love us with everything you are
holding us in your
eternal embrace
beloved cosmic matrix
from which I came
wrap me as a babe
in your blue robe of stars
rock me on your seat of wisdom
sing me your songs
of rose petals and justice
dance Christ's love into my bones
keep me, precious mother
cradled in your milky way
our lady of faith

may I walk the path of truth
that sets me free
teach me how to share your love
with my earthly family
blessed be
our mother of everyone
our lady of everything

~ Remothering ~

Are there places within you that feel as if they need
re-mothering?

We all have our stories of ways we feel we could have used better
mothering. Even if we had a good mom, chances are there are stories
we have made up about what we didn't get that we feel we need.

This is part of being an adult ourselves and doing our 'work' – to
name what didn't work. It's natural for us to identify places of neglect
or abandonment or a feeling of not being seen or heard. However,
there comes a time for all of us when it is time to stop blaming Mom
and deepen into the journey of mothering ourselves. In order to do
that we have to stop being a victim and may even need to let Mom
off the hook enough for us to do what needs to be done. Look at the
places which for you need re-mothering (hint: it is the places that you
may be angry with Mom about). Chances are you have already done
SO MUCH WORK around this and so this may just be one to move
past – but it might be just right.

Imagine that you are held and nurtured inside the arms of the
great, great Mother, a mother that will never depart from you, but
has always been there and will always be there. You don't need
to understand this concept to embrace it. Just let yourself SEE it
and FEEL this embrace. Dissolve into her embrace and even allow
yourself to feel trust. What does this bring up for you? Sadness?
Hope? Anger? Just let it come

(Perhaps read the poem again)

A People Who Believe

There are days
when it seems
life is too big for us
and no matter
what we dream up or
change we commit to making
it won't make the difference
to what we actually need.

As it turns out
it is not the change
itself we are in need of;
although, the critic
will always point
a crooked finger to that.
What we are in need of,
first and foremost,
is being a people
who believe change
is possible
even in the face of
the impossible.
And the ability to act
from that faith
instead of acting
from our despair.
We are destined
to rise and fail
and rise again
to love and hurt

and love again
to win and lose
and win again
to create and destroy
and create again.
It's just like that here on earth.

But I like it here.
I like the mystery,
this provocative,
buoyant bliss of existence.
As long as the poets can write about it
and the singers can chant about it
and the painters can paint about it
and the dancers can move about it
and the gardeners can plant about it
and the speakers can talk about it
and the lovers can make love about it
and the dying can praise it
and the living can live it
then. . . .

The world will continue
to turn round and round
and grace will dance with tragedy
like she has always done.

What we, the lovers of life
must do, and I do mean, must do,
is express ourselves and our passions.
Express our voices and our images,
as it is our very substance that keeps
the world from flying apart.

~ Don't Give Up ~

Where do you feel you have given up hope?

Is there some place in your own heart? Or life? Or relationship? Or even the earth itself? Is there a feeling of hopelessness about the state of things?

There are a lot of HSP's out here. Yep, that's Highly Sensitive Peeps, and HSP peeps have a hard time with all the bad news; it gets us down and for good reason. Things can look pretty crazy if we only look with outside eyes. You may wonder how to not give up when there is so much evidence to the contrary. It isn't that keeping hopeful will change outcomes, although it has been known to happen! It is rather that the outlook one experiences when one is willing to be unreasonable about hope and transformation creates vitality. The very energy of remaining optimistic changes the particles in the air, and in your body but you knew that already. And it isn't always so easy. Got that.

Then there is seeing what beauty there is to see that can help renew hope when we are down; see what is going right and use that as evidence to keep going.

Imagine being hopeful is bringing light to someone that needs it. See it going right from your heart to theirs. What does it feel like to be able to send love? Do you feel it instantly return to you? Who did you send it to? Pretend you can see the particles and waves moving in non-linear time. This love is quantum and you are connected to it.

Now imagine that you can give love to others without anything being taken away from yourself. This is different from protection since there is no need to guard.

Particle Prayer-making

Right at the edge of myself,
the place where I end
and you begin,
right there
in between
the particles we are,
there is another place.

A place between places
a space between spaces
where spirit and matter meet
and where the miracles
live within our reach
if we agree to reach

What are the thoughts
we haven't thought yet?
The ideas within our
consciousness that
although we have access,
we don't quite know
how to get into that field
where so much light
becomes available
and we can see into
the places we could not see into
just moments before

This field of possibility
is where the angels

extend their wings
and where stardust lingers
and we have a sense
it is here,
right now,
the divine intersecting
with the human

We are
You are
The Beloved is.

I will meet you there.
Because there is no place
I would rather be
than beside you
particle prayer-making
in the space between spaces.

When we go back
to our daily chores,
after visiting the mystical realm
and are renewed,
our faces sparkle with Heaven and
our family wonders where we've been,
even though we didn't even seem
to leave the kitchen . . .
the salty dough is still
being kneaded in our
capable hands.

For Sue Hoya,
The Mother of My Heart

~ Including Yourself ~

Do you see yourself as a part of everything that is?

Exploring the space between spaces is one of the favorite areas to hang out in for the Muse. There's less static there, less ideas of others, less BS that has accumulated. It is an internal wander land, a place to wander around inside and look around. Mostly we are looking for our own information there, but who knows what one might find.

Working within the vast realm of your creativity is like going to 'be a mystic' school for the ordinary person. Many of us don't go over there our whole lives, then when we do we discover how magical we really are. Not only that, it has been here all along – which could cause some upset for a while. You mean I could have had all this access to the other spaces and places all this time?

Imagine that access to your stardust in between veil spaces was easy. Close your eyes and just travel inside and see the sparks flying and the different colored fabrics rippling in the wind of change. Notice how your body feels as you go through spaces and places. See yourself as somehow integral to the spaces, not an outsider, but an insider. How would it feel if you were on the inside, freely accessing both worlds?

We are just cooling sacks of stardust.
We are asking the question, who lives in here?
This is our cosmic address.
We are already standing in the cosmos.

Sue Hoya Sellars

Source is Aware of Me

I live inside the awareness
that there is an ever-present flow of Divine Love
at all times, all around me.
This is the Source of my life, my substance.

Even when I am not aware of it,
my Source is always aware of me
and is working for good on my behalf.
Right in this moment, this love IS.

My path as a human being held in Divine Love,
is to practice releasing my fear and
make myself available to receive
and embody this abundant grace given freely.

Having the faith to allow myself to know and feel
I am held in the heart of the Beloved.
Sharing this love when I am inspired to do so,
and especially, when I am challenged to do so.

I count it as a gift to be able to discover
what my part is in the great unfolding,
and to live it to its fullness.
Which includes sharing this love with others.

It is my charge to expand my understanding
of myself, and this universe.
Offering my gifts on the altar of humanity,
I am invited to be a co-creative participant.

I am a part of the life of the Divine,
as the Great Mystery
unfolds its Great Story
upon this good green earth.

It is my joy to be in wonder of it all
and to find the awe in falling in love
with each day and this creation
and honoring it with acts of beauty.

May all beings
have the experience
of this
Big Love.

For SARK

~ Receiving Love ~

Do you make yourself available to love?

It is amazing how often we are blocking ourselves to ever present love. Perhaps we don't want to get hurt because we have been hurt before and feeling loved has led to suffering. Or maybe we don't think we are worthy of love, whether human or Divine. Or maybe we just don't feel it at all – even when we try.

Whatever the circumstance, this is an invitation to try something else, right now, and be open to becoming available to love. To let LOVE love you. This may be a foreign concept but it is time to bring it on home. Will you open yourself up to awe? Will you dare to just allow the love in? What is there to lose? You are a part of everything that is here, everything on heaven and earth. You matter and you are needed. Stop counting yourself out; get in here!

Imagine that there are no barriers between you and love. Start with seeing the barriers you do have; what color, shape and location do they have? How big are they, are they old or new or built by hand? Just be with them, then see LOVE dissolving them, particle by particle becoming more and more free and supple. Then imagine all the barriers are gone – and whoooooooshhhh the love just comes in. It could feel good – it could open your heart. It could fill you with radiance even for a second…

A Prayer for Artists

Our Lady,
Mother of All Good Things
We artists are a complex weaving.
Our beauty
and our suffering seek expression
through brush and pen
through hand and voice
through drum and dancing feet
through paper and scissor
through image and word
through color and form
through stars and sums
through hearts and minds
through lives and deaths
through desire.

We live drunk struck with joy
and fear struck with unworthiness.
Yes, fear enough to stay the brush
or halt the tambourine.

Is it worth it to make art?
Am I good enough? What is the value of my work?
What will others think of me . . . of it?
or cleaned my house after all,
Instead of getting myself to my studio
or my notebook for tea with the Muse.

This chatter poisons our ideas
with lack of Faith in the works of our hands.

As a form of medicine,
you have given yourself, Lady,
your own image and heart,
and holy flaming spark
to millions of painters, sculptors,
poets and songwriters.
This is why I am asking you,
the most painted Lady in all the world
on behalf of artists everywhere!
You are the most painted Lady in the world!
The most sung about Lady in all the world!
Lady, I beseech you on our behalf!
I call to you for the artists,
whose creative minds and hands and hearts
are set to something which is
LIFE GIVING.

Blessed Lady! Mother of All Good Things!
Hail, Holy Lady,
look upon our tribe of creative beings today!
Call us to the studio to light the candle!
Call us to the paintbrush filled with blue paint!
Call us to the piano filled with unsung songs!
Call us to the dance floor to dance with you.
And the anvil and the forging fire and crucible.
And the garden beds of red beet,
Gold plums and leafy greens.
Call us to the creative kitchen
where healing soups mend the world.
Call us to the streets
for spontaneous soul theater.
Call the poets to the cafés for readings again!

Call the writers to the desks
and set their pens on fire!
Call us to the blank canvas,
to find the messages within.
Call us to the uncarved block
to roll away the stone.
Call us to the camera
to capture children laughing
and to notice light of day.
Lady, the world is torn with
pain and grief and greed and yes we sensitive ones
feel the paradox and bring it to the studio for reckoning
Inform the artists it is our job to weave
our golden and red threads
through the dense matter of oppression
through the dark fog of injustice and the
tyranny of images sold which do not represent life
but the worst kind of death, the needless kind.
We cannot always do the saving of the world work
when we often need to be in the studio.
It is the prayer cubicle of the studio which
shows us how we too, can serve you in the
hurting parts of life.

Our creations are an antidote to the violence.
Artists are the revolutionaries who change
the world through provoking inquiry and possibility.
We are the visionaries who record
what 'they' do not want us to record
Our work is the work of truth telling,
the truths that come from the soul of the people
watching with the keenest of eyes.

And yes we struggle with worth and will!
And yes we shall proceed.

TODAY light the flame on our hearts and hearths
And cause an idea – a blessed spark of light
all the artists who choose to can feel and see
that flickering within us.
TODAY if we do not see or feel the spark,
or never feel inspired at all, STILL –
CALL US TO THE STUDIO!
Let us not wait for inspiration.
We create because we must –
To make art is to make life.

Call us, BLESSED MOTHER to remember who
We are – visionaries of the ages – whose work
keeps the balance in the unseen realms.
Our paintings count as prayers.
Hail, Full of Grace, hear my prayer
on behalf of all artist's everywhere,
I call to thee, Oh Holy Lady,
Most painted Lady in all the world.

For The Red Madonna Sisterhood,
and for Erin and Brianna

~ Valuing Your Creativity ~

Are you devaluing your creative process?

Sometimes our creativity can take the form of prayer, of supplication. Sometimes even a sense of desperation may arise, a request is making itself known in us. When we bring our self expression to this longing, creating in some way can take on a new value not only personally but collectively in our world.

Have you considered the contribution art makes in our world and in your own life? Consider the world without it, and yet we relegate it to hobby or an activity that happens when and if we have time or are inspired, instead of an essential part of our lives.

Imagine that making art was essential to your life, and really, to our world, that something would be lost if you weren't creating, that your creations were actually vital to the well being of others and your own sanity (true dat').

What do you think you would want to create? Are you drawn to painting, writing, dancing, teaching, weaving, pottery, acting? If you were creating as if your life depended on it, what medium would you choose next, at this point on your journey?

Imagine you are claiming yourself as an artist and turning that into a prayer. See yourself becoming alive with that idea, of the artist in prayer. What does it feel like? Look like? What do you see? If you were to paint it, what would it look like?

Tree of Life Blessing

May you choose outrageous actions
that challenge who you are
and encourage who you are becoming.

May you take one step, however small,
toward that which you have always longed for.
Now is the right time.

May you recognize the unique
and powerful contribution that you bring
to the people whose lives you touch.

May you be as wonderful as you really are,
and do things because you want to,
not just because you should.

May you celebrate your creativity
and believe you are an artist
with a unique vision that no one else has.

May you find peace and purpose
and possibility amidst the chaos,
while remaining aware of the unrest in the world.

May you reach towards the Spirit
with a longing that keeps you awake
to the miracles available all around you.

May your faith move any mountains
standing in your way and bring you
great teachers to awaken your understanding.

May you give up shame, guilt and self-neglect
and replace them with freedom, integrity, and
a path of self-nurturing.

May you offer the gifts and blessings of your soul
to beings of the world
when the time is ripe for you to release them.

May you passionately and deeply love
and be loved by someone
who can see who you really are.

May your body speak to you
and teach you how to care
for the temple housing your bright spirit.

May you walk gently on the earth
and honor your hearth and family
with your action and your rest.

May you find and enjoy the fruit of abundance
so that your life path
can be fortified and furthered.

May you embrace the Tree of Life
and be informed by the wisdom
She brings to those on Her path.

May LOVE be at the center of all your choices
and may you, with me,
send this blessing to all beings. Amen

For Havi Mandell

~ Receiving Blessings ~

Is there anything between you and allowing yourself to receive a blessing?

What if this very time was a time of allowing yourself to be blessed? To really receive the blessing of this life, and the bounty of this earth?

Receiving may be even harder than giving. There is a vulnerability in allowing ourselves to be blessed by others and the world, whether that is us feeling unworthy or just wondering about the application of the word itself – blessing. Blessings aren't something we deserve or earn or that are predictable, sometimes it is easier to think of them like grace and be thankful when we feel them.

Imagine that you are hugging the tree of life and it is hugging you back, that you are supported and held. What kind of tree is your tree of life? What does it smell like, feel like, look like? Are there blooms and flowers? What about the shape of the leaves or the roots? Receive oxygen from the tree as if it is a life transfusion. See that there is a place for you in the garden of life.

Receive the support and love available to you right now. Let it in, really in. This is not pretend, this is real, according to your feeling and imagination. Let it come to life in images – leaves, blossoms, fruits, beauty. You are beauty embodied. Remember, you are a blessing.

BONE GATHERING
Rants From Between Worlds

CHAPTER 5

Dear Reader,

This collection is drawn from the idea that each of us has sacred work and can choose it for ourselves. A sacred assignment. That there is a path or divine plan inside of us if we will listen to the call. There is work to be done in our inner world using our imagination and desire to go deep within.

As a woman entrepreneur, I find myself speaking to women entrepreneurs as part of my own sacred assignment. It takes a lot of work to get us to move into belief in ourselves. That we are worth the risk, and that our ideas may be blessings for the world, and also, work for ourselves and others.

I love to be in conversation about the concept of being visionary. I often represent the visionary in my paintings with the symbol of the winged eye, one who sees into the spaces between spaces. I believe that all of us have a capacity to be visionary, but we may or may not be working with that way of seeing and being.

I hope these poems inspire ideas to light sparks within the hearts of those who choose to bring the sacred path and sacred work together!

Signed in sparkling embers,

Shiloh Sophia

Visionary Work

The work of a visionary is
to know the past, dream the future
and take powerful action in the present.

We create a path where there are no paths,
lay groundwork where no ground lays.
We see behind the veil of impossible.

We do not follow the agenda
or the status quo or those *in the know*. No.
Our way is uncharted territory.

At the gateway where the worlds meet
you will find us gathered together
with a prayer for the possible.

The work of a visionary is
to know the past, dream the future
and take powerful action in the present.

~ Being Visionary ~

Where can you begin seeing the world with visionary eyes?

What does it mean to be visionary? Well, first of all, all of us are capable of it, and it clearly has roots in the word vision! In our story, it refers to a decision to 'see' things in a new and different way – and the Muse is VERY fond of seeing things in new ways.

When one is a visionary, there is also something inferred that suggests a seeing, not just for self, but for others and for our world, our planet, our species – seeing into the future of what others might not be seeing. Take a long view, or as the Native Americans talk about, making choices that are caring and considering the next seven generations.

It is visionary beings who would look beyond the current situation and choose sustainable choices and bring to life ideas that are ready for the here and now needs. A Visionary has a responsibility that often comes with deep seeing. Yet, often visionaries see the big picture and can become overwhelmed with all there is to be and do. That is why it is so important that we each unravel our own piece of the red thread, that which is ours to cause and create.

Imagine that you have wings on the side of your eyes that allows you to see what you cannot see with your ordinary eyes. What do your winged eyes reveal to you?

Heart of the Visionary

She is unreasonable about loving.
At the center of her being
is a heart as big and bright as the world.

She doesn't know how it got that way.
She knows a lot of women who feel
as she feels. Sensitive to energy and essence.

They want to save the world.
They want the suffering to end.
What is she to do, with all of this Love?
How can she love people she doesn't even know?

The lady at the supermarket.
The man at the gas station.
The little boy with dirt on his face.
The little girl with a flower in her hand.
The teenage boy working a night job.
The teenage girl feeling like she is not enough.
The old woman driving off the cliff after work one day.
The old man who daily walks his 3-legged dog.

This way of loving
changes everything about everything.
It is unreasonable to love unreasonably.

She remembers a time before they came.
Now she thinks of them as guests, but before
she thought of them as uninvited.

They have changed her.
The burden and bliss of an ever opening heart
has expanded her world.

She has been called a rebel.
A bitch. A mover. A shaker. A revolution-maker.
The guests of her heart call her to the road less traveled.

She walks between the worlds
Along the path, she sees what must be done.
Sees her part in the great unfolding.

Sees how she can soothe the suffering.
Sees the other visionaries on the path beside her.
Sees where she can go to make a difference

She recognizes that the way she serves
must be true to her own vision
in her own unique way, for renewal to continue.

She knows it isn't just selfless service.
She chooses the path of her generosity
based on where she feels called.
Love is at the center of all her choices.
Love for herself and love for others.
To the visionary, intentional giving opens access to a greater receiving.
She has been called to live from heart.
At the heart of the visionary is
the soul of the world.

For Shannon Shakti

~ Unreasonable Love ~

How spacious is your heart's capacity?

Many of us who care about the great unfolding of the universe feel a sense of responsibility for others. This may feel like an unreasonable love because it isn't rooted in knowing someone we know, but just this big huge spacious heart feeling. This can translate into great love that motivates us to act on behalf of others, where we feel a sense of unreasonable loving that lights up our heart fire and makes us want to take action, to serve, to live out our compassion.

This kind of loving can also translate into feeling too much, being too sensitive and not being able to act, as we are overwhelmed. We feel too much and we shut down. Our heart's capacity can even build up walls to keep loving out. Have you experienced this? We don't feel safe to be that exposed; in fact loving can feel like being naked or as if our skin is off. We cry at every emotional rage, and might even feel angry at the world, due to all the injustices. I mean we have a reason to be pissed.

Imagine, just for the moment that you are safe to love as big as you want, that you don't need to protect yourself. Notice what happens to your heart and body. Explore this a little at a time, not all at once, and practice feeling into it. Eventually it may expand. The heart has electromagnetic fields that expand for up to 20 feet – see those fields of color all around. Practice knowing this – especially when you are connected with others.

Bone Gathering

Returning to one's self
after a long voyage into the
desert, is the work all beings
must do one day.
The day will come when
the absence of the missing bones
and the pieces of your heart
you left on the highway to die
after too many mornings waking up
alone, in body or spirit or both,
will require you to return.

For this sacred work,
a map for returning will
be provided, so you can find
the missing persons' reports.
This map is not in a language
you will understand. *Are you surprised?*

With each stop on the quest
there may be a sitting-down-hard
head-in-hands-wondering-why
and even despair you thought
you had gone beyond.
Grief and wonder are the
companions you will find
because they are also the way
through the hard-to-see places.
Give in to them. You will be okay.

I wish I could say
it could be easier than this.
Hiding, cutting, dismembering
ourselves wasn't so easy, was it?
We did it to survive, we thought,
and we wrapped up the bloodied
limbs and continued on,
almost soldier-like in our sacrifice
of ourselves. Never mind the blood-loss
of not being ourselves.
Never mind not even knowing what song
belongs to our mouth and
what movement our body
loves the most.
How did we go on this way?
All that is done now.
No more, we say.
That is how we found ourselves here.
This excavation requires
specialized tools, if it didn't,
bone gathering would have started long before now.
Yes, I know you have already started.
I can see this in your tender eyes.

Don't worry. Yes, it is scary at first.
The tools are intact for user-friendly excavation
and you will find they fit your palm just so.

The stranger within you knows how to use each one.
She was the one yelling at you before,
to listen, listen, listen inside the soul cave
but now that you have listened to her,

she will be the one to help you see in the dark.
This is the one we call the Muse.

Visionary bones are made of stardust
and their sparks glow in the darkness.
Come. You will find them. You have to.
I need you to. I have gone a' bone gathering
I found this poem here in the red earth
and brought it to you for lighting.
Brush the dust from your feet
And you will find words dry enough
to ignite your embers.

For Lys Anzia

~ Gathering Fragments ~

What feels fragmented and ready to be called into togetherness at this time?

Many of us, since childhood, allow ourselves to be fragmented, taken apart, hidden, walled off, in the dark, under the bed. We may have promised ourselves we would be back – well maybe this moment is that moment. There is some shadow work to move through whenever we come to the place in our life when we realize how much of ourselves we have kept in hiding. Ouch. It can hurt the first time we see it. We may even spend time wondering how we could have allowed this to happen to ourselves. Pause a moment to just allow yourself to digest, yes, there has been a loss, but it doesn't have to continue to be a loss, because you can do the work of bone gathering.

Imagine that you can see and could name the primary parts of yourself that you want to call back. Perhaps begin with 2 or 3 (playfulness, innocence, open hearted) - just see what comes up for you. Then one by one call them back to yourself, and say the word, Then one by one call them back to yourself, like an invitation:

"COME! Joy, COME! Gratitude, COME!"

Your work won't be done quickly, but if you agree to do this deep work you will notice an expansion of your soul space. This would be great to sketch out – to make shapes of the 'bones' and fill them with your words. As you do this process, allow a sense of arrival.

The Creative Being Creed

My ideas are worth exploring
and my creative acts are sacred,
worthwhile and valuable.

I answer the call to create
without feeling I am taking anything away
from something or someone.

I know that I have something to say and create
that is only mine to express,
and so it is original.

I surrender the idea that my works of art
must be pretty, good or saleable,
and let them be what they want to be.

I consider the practice of creativity
equal to other practices like prayer or meditation
or exercise and I make time for it.

I share my creations
without needing or seeking
acknowledgement from others.

I release myself from the need
to feel inspired before I begin, trusting
everything I need to create will be provided.

I allow myself to release
the critic and perfectionist, with love
and invite the muse to come to my side.

I accept the healing energy coming
from my creative acts, I remind myself
it is okay to not know what I am doing,

Creativity is a journey,
and I honor this journey with my time,
my resources and my heart.

I am gentle with myself
when I haven't taken the time to create,
knowing I will begin again.

I give myself permission to be messy, loud,
irreverent at times, and at others
to be quiet, orderly, mindful and to feel blessed.

I am worthy of the title, Artist,
just because I create,
regardless of what I create, or the outcome.

I am free to think my own thoughts,
to have my own visions
I also gather nourishment from those around me.

I feel that my life is a great adventure
I am always looking for my full body YES
and choose to be just as clear on my 'No Ways.'

I believe in intentional creativity;
knowing the love I put into my work
goes out as a blessing towards that which is needed.

I am a creative being, not a creative doing,
and sometimes being creative is allowing myself
to do nothing except the act of dreaming.

I believe every bone in my body is a creative bone
I believe my life is a miracle in process
I believe that I am a creative being.

For the members of the Red Thread Café

~ Self Expression ~

Where do you feel a desire to be more self expressed?

Creativity isn't something for those who are considered talented or show promise as an artist. Those are illusions. Creativity is for everyone. Every bone in our body is a creative bone. You are a creation and you are creative.

Creativity is our natural self expression, that which helps us see who we really are. It is how we are designed; we are creations living inside of a created world. We can bring even more power to our creativity by bringing consciousness, intention, focus and power to it. Is there a part of your creativity that is longing for self expression? You don't need anyone else to tell you what is possible; choose to be a creative being because you are. Are you ready for that? Because it could get even more wild as your Muse begins to have her way with you. She may reveal unexpected surprises!

Imagine that you could be expressing yourself creatively in your life. What would that feel like? Imagine that you can see yourself being that way. What do you see? What do you long for? What medium? What area of focus or theme?

When you have some ideas, see a spark lighting up the darkness within . . . light . . . fire . . . passion! Is there an action you could take now that would allow you to engage with that energy? Consider this a dare to bring some creative fire into your life – really – not next month – how about now. Get a piece of paper and pen and begin to doodle, write, draw, see what comes out. Don't get in the way – let it flow out and then, see what it reveals to you.

Everything You Think You Know Changes

When everything you think you know changes
What do you do then?
When all that you dreamed you might cause,
you didn't end up causing,
What do you dream then?
When who you thought you were, isn't.
How then will you re-invent?
When how you believed the world to be,
deconstructs,
How shall you trust again?
When the ideas of childhood are no longer whole,
how do you reconnect to innocence?
When the instruction manual you thought you
understood and were following,
de-materializes,
what step-by-step do you follow?
When the life you thought you had is out of view,
how then shall you claim a new one?
When the paradigm you were living in
no longer makes sense,
how do you enter or make one
that matches who you are,
and where you belong
in the universe?
When your heart hurts
and the crack is opening even wider,
how do you continue to love and to listen?

Sigh. Heave. On your knees.
Soften your belly. Bellow. Roll.
Call your many mothers for help.
Listen really intently in between your cries.
Listen to the space between spaces.
The echo has information
you didn't see or hear before.
When the unraveling has begun,
you must just wait on the Beloved.
It will feel interminable.
Sit in the broken sanctuary,
even if the wonder and cries are so loud.
Know that you are not alone.
Don't try to get through it, get it done,
or rush to the next thing or to resolution
or the illusiveness of completion.
Don't make up new stories
to go in the place of the old ones, yet.
Sit in the discomfort and
the spaciousness of not knowing.
There is an absolute everyday reality
that all of us will one day
find ourselves face down
inside of the broken sanctuary.
Don't make finding yourself here wrong.
Light from your wounds will emerge.
Watch for the tender rays of fragile beauty.
This is what you have been looking for.
What you left behind and
what you gathered up.
This is where light comes from.

~ Informed by Beauty ~

Do you allow beauty to inform you?

Beauty is all around us all the time as a form of medicine. That is part of how we can heal ourselves when we choose to let it in through our senses, to see it, feel it, know it, hear it, allow it to infuse us. Our senses hold many clues to wellness.

This takes a kind of willingness to allow beauty in. Strangely we are often blocking it!

For many, viewing art and listening to a fine piece of music and literature that is brilliant, helps us not only heal, but to feel less alone. In the case of many great minds and hearts, their work actually counters the status quo, accepted norms, and standards. Strangely we are often blocking it! Many have the impact of squashing beauty in an effort to normalize.

Beauty allows us to be re-enchanted with the world.

Imagine that you are watching a body of water, and that there are diamonds of light sparkling on the water. Each diamond of light goes in through your eyes and brings that light into your body as beauty. Imagine you are a body of sparkling beauty. Sit with this energy. When you are ready, let that light spill back out of you and back into the body of water. May you walk in beauty dear one!

This Work of Women

Yes. It is time for a revolution
of women and path,
women and money,
women and business,
women and art,
women and marketplace.
We do not choose
to give away our works for nothing.
We are not starving or frivolous artists.
We are creators whose creations save lives,
heal the world, mend wounds.
This work of women, priestesses and practitioners
of every kind is
VISIONARY WORK.

Our work is vital. Essential. Needed.
This work of women must include creating livelihood.
This is not easy, quick, fun or likely.
This is not accepted or encouraged.

But this is what we must do:
Create an abundance revolution.
Create our own path.
Create our own money.
Create art.
Create our own marketplace.
We must be compensated.

We are creating our own mystical cosmic
luminous overflowing BANK.
A bank that does not cause, contribute or condone
the suffering of others for profit.
A women's bank.
Believe it. Create it.
Deposit into it. Draw from it.

Invite other women into it.
Enter the income stream in your little golden boat
and dream and work and pray
and play and
do not stop.
Keep going.

It will seem impossible.
But we will make miracles.
Miracles are organizing themselves
around our dreams,
our work,
right now.

~ Inviting Abundance ~

Where do you feel like you want to bring abundance into your experience?

There are, of course, many kinds of abundance: physical abundance, the abundance of the universe, and the state of your mind, heart and body. All work together to bring an overall experience of abundance. We can have abundance and not see it, or we can have very little and choose to see it as abundance.

So much of living in abundance has to do with how we choose to see and work in the world, our actual framework for how we view ourselves and others. Choosing an abundant outlook is often the first step in creating it. Consider for a moment what your actual outlook is. What are your views? Is the universe an abundant place? Is the world filled with takers more than givers?

Imagine that you have a golden touch. That through your touch you have the capacity to alchemize your area of focus into gold, meaning something more bountiful than it was before your attention. What would you choose to turn into gold in your life, in the world, and in the lives of those you love? Consider doing some journaling about being at cause for inviting your own abundance – and enjoy the process as you open to a new flow of energy and ideas!

A Free Thinking People

This is freedom. That I might think the thoughts
which I would like to think.

Free from the frames of thinking
I may have taken on.

To have a free thought
in which my own mind is Queen.

How might we disentangle ourselves
from the consumer construct?

What is the method by which we will unveil
the thoughts that bind us?

Especially the ones
we do not even know are there?

Our job is to break out of this prison of thought.
So that we may think our own thoughts.

~ Releasing Limitations ~

Where do you feel caged in? Our self imposed cages are the worst ones because they are the ones that we keep in place either with our will, or because we don't even know they are there!

It's kind of crazy that way; we are held, trapped, entangled in our own webs long after others have stopped caging us, we remain. Why is that? First we have to know they exist.

Do ideas come to mind for you instantly, symbols or images or even captors from the past? When we say we feel stuck, held back, hemmed in, these are all metaphors. Metaphor means to cross over, so these symbols help us articulate something that is rather invisible, like a self imposed cage. We use metaphor to keep it in place and can use metaphor to liberate it.

Imagine yourself inside of the cages you have created, which are often represented by actual beliefs or stories you have invented. See them in your life. What is it that you see? Is there one big one and what is it made of from a material standpoint – steel, other people's ideas, smoke and mirrors? Whatever the material substance of your primary cage of thought, you are invited to see it shape shift and dissolve.

As it dissolves, imagine that you are free, liberated from that cage. Then, most importantly, don't go back in. You can do that by creating a new belief that you are already free.

Do You Choose or Are You Chosen?

Do you choose, or are you chosen?
Do you make the path
or has it been in you all along?
The soul's journey deepens at the crossroads.
There is nothing else to do.

Say Yes.

All steps now
are about staying on the path
which has chosen you.
Your path will call upon
everything you think you are.
And show you
day-by-day
moment-by-moment
the mystery of the great and bountiful
wild sacred self you have always known
Let Her out.

~ Choosing the Path ~

Do you you have a path? Do you create it or is it destiny?

When one feels like they are on a path there can be a profound sense of purpose, being on task, and even arrival, even though there is a journey taking place. When we don't feel like we are on a path we often say yes to things that should be a no, and no to things that could be a yes and more in alignment with who and how we feel. The difference of being on one and not being on one is quite illusive unfortunately. The difference is simply your decision to be ON THE PATH and identify it and where you are, and if inspired, to even name it. Sure, some just have that sense of feeling called, but don't leave the joy of being on a path to those who already know they are on it! This is your choice, your right, and will allow you to flow more freely in the proper direction.

Imagine that you are already on your path. Yes, right now you are there. Look down at the path you are standing on, see your feet there. What color is the path, what material; see the visuals that compose the very path itself. Then see your feet begin to walk forward . . . is there any language for what you are experiencing? You don't need to ever not be on your path again. Claim it. This is a daring adventure, claim your journey!

DANGEROUS TERRITORY

Cosmic Cowgirls Campfire Songs

CHAPTER 6

Dear Reader,

This collection is in honor of my tribe, and sparked by the magic held in our community, the Cosmic Cowgirls. We are women who walk between worlds, bringing the holy, sacred parts of ourselves into companionship with the irreverent wild free part of ourselves. The result is often unexpected when we discover we aren't who we thought we were. Many members of our community feel like they are from somewhere else, as if they aren't from around here. There are many stories of not belonging or thinking one came from outer space somehow and waiting for your real family to come pick you up.

Perhaps you are one of the ones who got dropped off at the wrong family. When we explore our deep complex inner creative world we often encounter someone we relate to as the mystic badass - an internal archetype that is no longer willing to take any sh*t. She wants to weave truth and fiction and poetry from the strands of the mystery and discover something that she has never seen before, but has always felt.

To do this, we have to agree to open the doors that have no keys and see what has been waiting for us all this time. The powerful thing about this is that when you do awaken - you get well enough to be a blessing to others, to make a contribution to the collective and to share your own messages of magic, madness and muses at the back door of the heart.

Signed with the fire of the Phoenix,

Shiloh Sophia

La Puerta

I am calling upon the name
the very sound that opens the door
to the world inside
where the miracles mend and knot
endless red threads for me.

Where that which the Divine has sparked
Lights up the openings
Which I am here to cause and create!
Not needing one more particle
of time or money or kin or purpose
in order to reach inside and pull forth
the shining strands of truth.
I reach, I call, I push, I press, I seek,
I pray, I hold, I bless, I cry, I trust
in the unknown, unresolved, unspoken.
I believe goodness is my real religion
that which seeks to heal and hold,
bless and anoint,
that which seeks to mend
the tattered souls within us,
and is called toward beauty
and shuns that which no longer serves.
I call upon the door: Open!

~ Being Ready ~

Where in your life is ripe for action?

There is so much in our lives that longs for us to show up for it and take action, to move, to manifest, to say yes. We hesitate, hem and haw, and wait for circumstances to improve.

Yes, there is something to say for prudence and timing but often we aren't daring enough and blame it on caution. This is how we think we are keeping ourselves safe. And for a time it actually appears as if we are, but that back fires soon enough and the safety places can even become places of danger where we have been holding ourselves back.

Imagine the areas of your life represented like colored doors. Pick three: what colors are they and what is the word on each of the doors? The areas that show up will be the ones you choose to open – ready or not!

Allow yourself to be surprised at what doors show up. Now narrow your focus and pick just one to walk through. Let the colors on the front of the door light up so you know which one to move towards. Then . . . OPEN SESAME! (Says me.)

A Flock of Phoenix

This is the time
when women and sacred work
rise and fly together. The Phoenix.
Adorned in fire red and diamonds
ready to fly to her next destination.

We have worked the whole time.
We knew our work was valuable
even when we were told it was not.
Some of us got lost in knowing
but not knowing what to do about it.

That is finished now.
A new chapter is being written.
A new prophecy is being called out.
Women are wise. Women are abundant beings.
We stand for each other and beside one another.

We, who are able, must rise.
And make space for others to rise.
Each of us makes up her own fire rising song.
We sing the words into creation.
Causing new creations to spark.

Just because there was a time
when fire was used against us
does not mean we gave up fire.
No. We have breathed fire,
taken it into our being. We are hot.

Our legend is not only one of burning.
Our legend is one of fire dancing.
Of choosing to burn
and then choosing to rise.
Sometimes the nest was burnt in the process.

The earth in her wisdom pushes us from beneath.
The air in her understanding nudges us upward, calling.
Up we go. Free at last.
Leaving gravity to its daily chore
of holding all things in place.

But not us. Not today.
Today, we soar.
If you were to look up, you will find
a sky full of radiant fire red birds.
A whole flock of Phoenix Women.

Together, we fly on the wisdom
and formation of the shared flock.
Sharing in the sacred work and ways we have gathered.
Bright and beautiful. Impossible and full of audacity.
Rise oh Winged Sisters and claim our skies!

For My Sister Shannon, the Cinnamon Cowgirl

~ Rising Up ~

What are you choosing to transform from repressed or encaged to flying free?

The Phoenix story has many legends associated with it that are powerful teaching tools when we identify them. Let's look at a couple of things: 1) she chooses to burn her own nest and 2) rises from her own ashes. Particularly for women, this pattern of burning and rising is familiar and can be extremely powerful when used in service of chosen transformation.

Imagine that you are the one starting the fire of your own nest, because it is time. What does the nest represent for you? For many it may represent moving onto a new phase of life, letting go of past relationships or ways of operating, divorce, an empty nest, an over-giver who now chooses to take care of herself first.

Once you see the nest, go ahead and set metaphoric fire to it through the heat of your gaze; really look at it and tell yourself the truth about it. See it for what it is and choose to let it be transformed in the fire of love. See the flames! Now imagine others who also had to burn their nest. Think about them and the collective quality of what you chose as your nest. Send love out to anyone who is ready to move on, who can't seem to find their way. Then when you are ready, dust yourself off and rise up. Perhaps this is a time to call a party, with others celebrating this transformation!

Endless Quest

I woke up knowing
what I knew
but knowing it newly:
There is no true
language for this.

Though our poetry
tries the mightiest pen
upon this particular page and honors
this endless quest with eager words
that can serve no justice.

Listen now to what we already know:
The places that ache in us the most
are not the ones named
for someone or something known
but something unknown in us.

Our disbelief of being missed,
not seen, not heard, not known.
Our desire to be known
for longer than an hour or a day.
Our ache to be witnessed
as we long to witness ourselves.

Beneath the shame and lack of self-love,
childhood stories, deaths, divorces
and dream-dashed days,

beyond the endless quest
for a romantic beginning
and ending to the story.

There lives in us
a knowledge of true self
never ceasing
to want to make itself seen.
A desire to be known.

~ True Self ~

Where do you feel that you are not seen? Are there certain situations or relationships?

There is no one who doesn't want to be seen. Especially when we have woken up to ourselves, to beauty, and to what is possible when we are deeply seen by others. Not being seen in our relationships is maddening and we can become quite irritable and pissed off! It can become a pursuit.

Here's a hint though; people who aren't awake to themselves have a hard time seeing others. However, if you are awake enough and you choose to see someone who cannot see themselves, there is a chance of sparking their awakening.

Imagine that you have eyes that have the power to truly see others and that seeing them, has them wake up. See yourself as that person, who through your eyes of love, acknowledges others into their own awakening. Is there anyone you want to reach out to?

Consider this a dare. Walk around all week looking at people and seeing them. Even if and especially if they haven't learned to see themselves or you yet. See what happens.

Dangerous Territory

We are a tribe of truth tellers.
Revolution makers.
Movers and shakers
of things that need moving
and shaking. Like hips.
And old ideas in need
of shaking off.

We are a gathering of women
who straddle the worlds.
We have one bare foot on the earth
(toenails painted sparkly of course)
And one cowgirl boot on the dancefloor.
With our heads in the stars for big dreaming
and our arms outstretched
to embrace as much aliveness as we can.
We have our flaming hearts on our sleeves
Whether we be sinners or saints
or wear halos or horns there is
one thing you have to admit about us . . .

We think for ourselves.
There is never a something better
than the you that is you.

Here, where the Cosmic Cowgirls
reign, we agree:
Be the most you that you can be.
Whoever that is for you - and we,
the sisterhood of the cosmos,

will hold your hand
as you molt on the dance floor of life.
Then we will clean up the first layer of
your skins and feathers for you
and most likely,
we will hoot and holler for you –
or meditate quietly -
or beat the drum.

We choose our own
rites of passage around here.

We believe this truth to be self-evident:
The pursuit of identity
is essential to the quality of our aliveness.
That each woman can transform
her life into a legend.
Stories are made for telling
around the campfire,
but legends are meant to be lived.

Sisterhoods are meant to
be our bridge when we don't know
the way over the troubled water
of the lies we have been told
and tell ourselves still.

Legends are not hatched.
They are concocted. Brewed. Stitched.
Woven together with time, friendship
red thread, spit, blood and tears.

For the Cosmic Cowgirls

~ Belonging ~

What's your story about how you got here?

We all have a story about how we got here, whether that is how we were conceived or our mother's pregnancy journey or how we were delivered. As it turns out, that story is greatly affecting all of our relationships because we are operating from that worldview. It happens so young, before our consciousness is able to choose something for a lifetime; it chooses what it can in the moment to help you survive.

For most of us, we are operating out of survival even when we no longer need to be. Then we bring that out into our relationships and choices for work and creativity. Can you see your survival story?

A wonderful thing can happen when we stop surviving only and enter into the space of belonging, but do we get to just choose to belong? It isn't that easy, but it always starts with the awareness of the story we already have operating.

Imagine that you do belong, that there is somewhere you can call home, that a circle is surrounding you that supports you in being who you are, without silencing your voice. See yourself as being connected to a tribe on earth. It does exist. Consider this a dare - that you reach out to others that you admire, and invite yourself into their circle.

Unfold Your Own Legend

A legend is composed of fact
and fiction and poetry.
It is our business what
Combination we choose to express.

We are not static. We are not a brand.
We are evolutionary beings,
cyclical, mutable, changeable
and relentless explorers of
the luminosity found in the inner
and the outer-ness of existence.

We can explore ourselves
with searchlights to discover
the voice inside this vessel of self.
What are these jewels I find inside
that no one ever told me existed?
When is it my time to shine?

We are a tribe of dissidents and misfits.
Bad ass rebels and myth makers.
Our job is clear and a new culture is created:
We invite you to uncover your own truth.
We show you the tools for excavation:
story, song, stroke, sift, swing, squeal, shimmer.

Don't worry
Our tools don't homogenize your revelations.
For a time when you are tender,
you might look and feel more
like *one of us* than you will later on.

In the myth making workshops hosted here
the crafting of a new self takes time.
This is not because you are
being absorbed, this is because
we are sheltering you inside
of our legends and truths
while you find your own
and learn to wield them like swords.

We will be here to notice
the sparkling parts of you emerging.
We will say - my, look at how
shiny her coat is, and how strong her gait.
We will invite you to life as the great adventure
instead of a story that happens to you.

We may hand you
a paintbrush, a writing pen, a drum
a fiddle, a magic wand, a bar of dark chili chocolate,
some cowgirl boots, a jar of gold glitter and
a ball of red thread and the craft of inquiry . . .

Creativity, curiosity and inquiry into oneself is
the daily cup of tea, here with the Cosmic Cowgirls
live from the Red Thread Café
where no guilt sandwiches are ever served,
and the door to the heart
is always open.

For Carmen Baraka, Spirit Warrior

~ Healing Your Story ~

What primary story is running your life?

Each of us runs our life through story. Things happen and we make up stories about them. Life is a series of stories that eventually shapes our identity. Each story has recurring patterns based on who we are. Those patterns over time ebb and flow the shape of the container for who we are until we kind of 'become' a series of responses to our story.

We are often trying to prevent more bad things from happening to us, if we have been hurt, which we all have, and meanwhile we are also preventing love from coming in. The same thing that protects, can also block. We begin to limit our story to keep ourselves safe. Adventure, appears to be too risky for the identity we are now attached to. We want to keep a firm grip on our story so that we don't lose ourselves. Then we can get smaller and our world gets smaller; to fit the pictures we have created. We all know how this turns out. No room to grow and become what wants to happen next. We get caught up in the living and miss out on the loving.

Imagine that you get to invent your own story and that you are a part of a very important and sacred circle. Others are gathered who have important information for the world. You have a place there and soon it will be your time to speak…what will you say? See yourself saying it, find your words. And see what you are wearing as you share your own medicine!

Legendary People Are Everywhere

Legendary people are everywhere.
Not all of them think of their life that way.
All of us are living out an amazing story.

Sometimes the bad stories keep infecting
the good stories and we find it hard to
have a sense of wholeness.

We can become fragmented by holding
everything that has happened before:
it weighs on us and pokes us in the eye.

No closet is big enough and our heart
is not the place to store bad stories.
There are other ways.

Good stories, the ones we invent, and love,
the ones we want to keep and continue
are what we are after.

Good stories are powerful enough to
transform bad stories into something useful.
This takes making a decision.

You might find yourself saying,
"I will make use of all my tragedy
and put it to work on my behalf,"

If you can recognize that the most
truly interesting people
also had a challenging childhood.

Interesting people also hurt someone important
also took what did not belong to them
and still need to say I am sorry.

No one has it all figured out
everyone has dark secrets, no one is alone in their quest.

Good stories need room to grow.
and soon the bad stories
will be put into a useful context.
Your life is a living witness to this.

Look around.
Legendary people are everywhere.
And you are one of them.

~ Being Legendary ~

Do you feel that there is a myth you are waiting to unfold?

Around the Cosmic Cowgirls we say that legends are composed of fact, fiction and a little bit of poetry. The legend we create is indeed based on our actual stories and our interpretation of them, but also making those stories into something fun to live and tell. These stories bring an air of creativity, fancy, and of tales told around the campfire of the heart.

If we choose to be the one who creates a legend, then we are choosing to be at cause for the creation of our story in this life. The outcome for this life is going to be quite different than if we allowed the story to just happen to us. So if you invent the legend you want to tell and you imagine it even as a tall tale, something that hasn't yet happened, what comes to mind for you? What would you like to say happened on your watch? What would feel exciting to live out? What is calling to you to be created?

We get to choose to be engaged with life, to be an inventor, to choose the archetype we live within, and we get to choose to do impossible things. Legends are invented; they don't just happen. Although everyone is legendary, only some of us will actually create a legend.

Imagine that you are going to create your life as a legend. What would it sound like? Throw some adventure and mystery in for good measure. Weave in a little fiction too and see what kind of good trouble you can get yourself into!

A Blank Canvas is a Door

When approaching the blank canvas
imagine that it is a door.
A portal of possibility in
which only you hold the key and the magic words
which grant access.
A cosmic opening which is beckoning you to enter.
Consider that what lies just beyond that white space
might just be the stuff of genius.
The empty canvas is used by the Muse
to terrify, entice, compel, repel, shake us in our boots!
And often, faced with it's blank face, we turn back.
But not today.
Today we choose to enter the unknown,
to answer the call which silently and powerfully
transports us from this present reality
into non-ordinary reality.
Now be brave and lay aside:
what we think we know
what we are sure we don't
and we might just experience
something close to bliss.
We may find that, yes, mind can quiet,
even without being a yogi or meditating for years.
Creativity calms even with chaos.

Pick up a paintbrush and empty your fears
into a palette of infinite possibility.
Postpone inviting that familiar critic to tea,
(the muse won't have any use
for her rough medicine today).
Tears may come . . .

and if they do, let them fall onto the canvas.
Terror may come . . .
and if it does, choose its color carefully and watch
as each stroke transforms and moves.
The Muse may come, and if she does,
let her have her way with you,
don't hold back,
or shield your heart
from her powerful strokes.
How long has it been since we burned with passion?
How long have we waited
to make our mark on canvas or page,
holding oh so many stories inside?
Today approach that blank canvas
remembering it is not about being good or pretty.
Today be a willing fool for creativity.
At each moment, surrender.
surrender. breathe. surrender. breathe.
Self expression is the key to unlocking a life,
not just the white door of your canvas.
Self expression is the you that lives inside
being invited into the world of form . . .
Just see what will happen
if you let yourself out in full color,
unconcerned with blend, contrast,
perspective or perfection.
Let this be one of the places in your life
where your fear
and your magic mix – POW!
That giant brush in your hand
wreaking havoc on your old ideas –
WHOOSH!
And creating space for something entirely
new to emerge: YOU, in living color.

~ Re-invention ~

What is ready for re-invention? A new space and place? A new view of what's possible?

Inside of each one of us there is a desire for something new, a blank canvas or a blank page to begin again, a chance to re-invent. We long for it; it wakes us up at night; our soul is trying to speak to us. Will we listen?

The blank canvas is a metaphor for the potential of a new story, one you invent based on what and who inspires you, your desire, instead of just your default story.

Imagine that you get this chance of a blank canvas to re-invent your life and you get to choose what goes into it. What would you include? What dreams? What relationships? What desires?

Maybe you will be brave and face your creative fears. Go get a new canvas and make your mark. What is the shape of re-invention?

The Alchemist's Brush

In pursuit of the intangible magic
that converts "base" into beauty
you approach the canvas with awe.

You wonder how you got here.
And why it took you so long. It feels like you were called.
Fear grips you as you stare into the unopened opening.

Your canvas, that permeable membrane.
A physical place representing and holding space
for the world between worlds that you seek.

How can it be that this grace is yours,
that without earning your place here at this threshold
the "in between" becomes available? Freely given.

Freely given to gifted and novice one and all.
This work is not just for the talented or gifted;
it belongs to all beings who dare to wield the brush.

Yes. This is your moment of reckoning and release.
No philosopher's stone encoded to confound.
The canvas will become your philosopher's stone.

No secret codex or symbol or faith grappling from
someone else's story of old or new or now. Just. You.
And. This. Cosmic Moment called: Painting.
Shall I say that word again, that which has become
honey to the tongue of the bitter?
That has opened the way to becoming?

Painting. Image making. Symbol gathering.
Intentional creating. Prayer making. Story healing.
Self renewing painting.

Overcoming voices that taunt and torture,
a new voice begins to emerge that is your own
and she asks you to release birds from cages.

You, with your heart and hopes ablaze, take that which
has need of transformation to that portal of possibility
and make your mark.

Marking out your intention onto that canvas with
fierce flaming tips and smudges of charcoal and tears.
You become alert. Engaged. Awe ensues.

You listen to requests for chalices to hold elixirs
and flowers for hair and mantles of red thread to wear.
She asks for new territory to explore, old stories to end.

She asks for you to listen . . . here inside of you.
She shows you the alchemical domain where the future
unfurls her legends.

That which is written in your bones is released,
begins to light up the sky.
Who is that star streaked wonder?

Yesterday's stories become tomorrow's material
for pulling strands of pure pigment from the edges of
wounds and somehow, yes, making magnificence.

This image begins to emerge
that now defines you for you
instead of someone else's view.

In a blink of stardust from a winged eye . . . You. Feel.
Different. What was that? Could that be healing itself?
Could this be true medicine?

An antidote to the violence within?
A voice of vision breaks the sound barrier.
Can you hear it? See it? Feel it?

Breathe. Stroke. Swirl. Sing. Sway. Swish. Call out.
Call in. Cast out. Caress. Renew. Reshape. Remember.
Reveal. Resound. Humbled. Praise. Arms raised.

Indistinguishable from prayer
the name of the Divine parts your lips
without known consent.

Walking a sacred path requires practice and
you knew this, but perhaps you were yet to find your method
for weaving that call within to make it manifest

The canvas has become the shape of the container
into which you pour the contents of your stories and visions.
And the context?

Oh yes, the context is: This is soul work.
Your body has knowledge of this sacred rite.
Being that we too were made in the Divine Image.

This longing to create in one's own story and image
has been passed down from ancestors who painted birth and
bison on cave walls. Icons of family life.

There is a deep remembering rising up now within you.
Access is finally granted to the story chambers.
Enter with the tenderness of an archeologist.

You look inside the cave of self.
Haven't you heard? Brushes are magic wands.
Giving language and form to the unspoken.

Through this creation, lives are opened.
The alchemist's brush continues her sacred work
with the fire of your heart as crucible.

From the shadows of self you reveal your gold
and the embers of your soul fire glow
and extend possibilities to the world.

For the women of Color of Woman

~ Intentional Creativity ~

What energy within you is ready to be alchemized?

What it means to create with intention is powerful beyond measure, bringing ourselves into tandem with the quantum world. To bring our mind and heart and soul and body into the task of creating with a specific inquiry in mind - is to say I am ready to move energy with my thoughts, actions and brush strokes. When we bring our whole selves, including all that we are dealing with, to the present moment and move them through color, light, symbol, story and inquiry, then we are offering ourselves up for the fire that changes us. Creating, with paint and word - really any medium, allows for energy to be moved in ways we cannot just move with our mind. Stuck particles begin to lose their position and fly around, moving out of pattern and creating an opening.

Imagine that each of your stories has an energetic pattern in your field, the field which is around your body like an egg of colored light. See if there is a story that wants to be alchemized in the fire. Where is it located in your field and how long has it been there and are there any messages it wants you to know? After listening, invite it to MOVE from where it is, to be alchemized into light. POOOOF. Consider this a dare, to be different than you were just moments ago. Release attachment to that pattern. What do you notice?

Is your Muse calling you towards something?

LICK THE FIRE
Dares of the Muse

CHAPTER 7

Dear Reader,

There is something about working with images and language that feels dangerous – like walking the edge of a self you don't yet know. You may feel called to ideas that go bump in the night, or not.

Many of these writings are counter-intuitive, and even reject common views of trust, innocence, and access. Moving through veils to see the hidden doorway to the hidden room in the soul where all the juiciness is taking root in the darkness.

I mean it is so popular to trust yourself and trust the process, but often, we don't, the key is really to proceed without needing to trust simply because we feel called. There inside of that place, there is a riddle to unknot that has been waiting for your attention.

It isn't about you taking on these ideas or views, rather, about you considering the views you hold of your assumptions and ideas, and setting fire in the darkness.

Stirring the pot of discontent. Seeing what no longer needs to be there that was propping up the old ideas and the old life. Shaking free of assumption and taking a deep dive into the mystery.

Signed in the curvature of riddles and milk from the milky way....

Shiloh Sophia

I don't trust myself

I don't trust myself
because my heart is unpredictable.
I don't always do what is best for me.

I follow a red thread where it leads
even if it is into dangerous territory
where there is no map in hand.

I don't trust myself
because I let my mind wonder and wander
into places I should not visit after dark.

The thrill of *what could be discovered*
keeps me awake at night
wanting. Something. But what?

My Muse is irrational and emotional
and she makes me do things good girls
should think twice about.

My heart is cracked in many places
and the pale yellow light sometimes
casts an eerie hue over my choices.

I don't want to be hurt again
yet I am willing to be fully wrecked.
Bring it on.

I live in unreasonable love and risk.
I thrive on not knowing
and sometimes moving forward, not trusting.

Trusting keeps me safe.
I don't want to risk being too safe.
Safety sometimes blocks possibility.

I don't trust myself
because I haven't yet unfolded
and I don't know how I will turn out.

What if I fall?
Indeed, I can trust I will fall.
Falling in love is always a risk worth taking.

Do I know aliveness counts more
than almost anything?
Yes. I do.

Do I trust this process?
No. *Of course not.*
It isn't required after all.

If I could know the outcome,
and trust how it would turn out,
then I wouldn't have nearly as much fun.

I wouldn't have nearly as many
mind-heart-opening-blowing-open-wide-days
and openings to unseen ways.

With skinned elbows, cracked heart
and ready pen to capture poetry from the
underside of stones in the bottom of the river.

I set out.
No matter where I end up
I know I have journeyed.

Can I count on myself for the truth?
Only sometimes.
That will have to be good enough.

I can trust this:
Creation is the key
to everything there is.

And so you will find me
in my studio today
creating, risking, failing.

Not trusting myself one bit
and having a grand time.
You should try it sometime.

This trust thing isn't all
that it is cracked up to be.
Try risking everything for love.

~ Self Trust ~

In what ways would you like to set yourself loose?

We are so hard on ourselves, so often trying to make ourselves lovable and dependable. Respectable even. Then we lose that wild edge that keeps us in the mystery. We are constantly trying to get stable, when perhaps getting less stable will upset the apple cart enough for something else to happen.

Our desire for dependability can make us predictable, to the point of cliche – and our desire to look good can keep us from letting ourselves loose. If you stopped trying to impress others and yourself and you just let loose, what do you think would happen?

Imagine yourself as free, a bird flying over the ocean. See yourself just free to fly, without attachment or outcome or needing to impress or meet a deadline. How does that feel in your body, in your soul?

As for the dare, are you willing to find more ways to be free in your life? What would that look like for you? Will you dare to be more free? If you don't know what that looks like or feels like then it is hard to imagine it –try it.

Territory of Belonging

We believe in living
in the in-between spaces.
Of not arriving. Of not knowing.
Of honoring the mystery.
Oh sure! We are all about
claiming our destiny
but, we know on the
way to claiming, there
are many valleys of tears
and quiet and wonder
and tiredness and awe
at how things have not quite
turned out as we had planned.

In time, new ideas and connections
will light the divine spark again.
Concoctions will begin to bubble.
Stories of hope, daring,
compassion, adventure,
kinship, creativity, invention,
freedom, sisterhood, possibility.
Poetry and miracles are the
cultural vocabulary of our tribe.

When all your stories
have been told
your legends begin
to unfold.
Friends hold you
through them and to them.

We believe there is medicine,
sacred and true, in community.
It comes with the
territory of belonging.
Of being a part of something
bigger than you. And me.
A place where the collective soul
can unfurl her wings and
together we can fly
into a future that reflects
who we are
and what we care about.

However. I must give you a warning:
if you enter *Cosmic Cowgirl Territory*
there is no way your wild woman
will keep herself contained.

Beware of shifting stories,
and old ideas falling away.
Beware of taking up space;
making others uncomfortable
is just part of this gig.
Beware of no longer being
willing to live a life
that does not reflect
who you are.
This is dangerous territory. *Welcome.*
Your cup of revolutionary tea
with the Muse is waiting for you.

For Ti Klingler

~ Adventurous Soul ~

Where does your soul long take you?

We rush to grow up, settle down, get things in order. We put off adventure until a better time. And there is no question that this kind of life feels good – and safer.

But the soul may long for something other than that, and we may not be willing to let our soul lead us. We may find ourselves becoming restless and longing for something we don't have language for. What do we do then? Do we shrink back and wait for something to appear, or do we go out and seek adventure?

In searching for what you long for, consider that which you deeply love. Sometimes adventure is correlated to what we love that is wanting our attention, love in that we desire it, want it, hope for it, dream of it.

Imagine, just for today, that you could go on an adventure trip planned by your soul for you. Where would she take you and what would she see? Who would go with you and why? What would you wear? What would the destinations be? Would it be abroad or inside your own soul?

Consider this a dare to take one action towards the adventure that awaits you. . . .

Meet Me in The Shimmering

Consider
that there is a thought
you haven't thought before.

Consider that you have access to
material living within you
that you didn't know you had access to.

Consider there is a great abundance
open to you all the time
that you have yet to discover and explore.

Consider there is an elegance
in your inner language
your mouth has yet to form words around.

Consider there is soul calligraphy inside
longing for a brush to stroke it to life
with astute tenderness.

Begin to wonder . . . what if you are not
who you think you are? This could be a relief.

Begin to wonder . . . what parts of you
might become available if you
honored yourself with creative acts?

Who are you not being? What are you not seeing?
What is the tired story wanting to be
transformed into a revolution from within?

When you have a connection
to the you that is you, the whole world appears
and occurs differently, doesn't it?

Yes, it does. The Muse lives here.
Let's spend time in that place
where the worlds meet. Shall we?

We become more of who we truly are
simply through our willingness to
show up in the shimmering.

For Jenafer Joy

~ Accessing Within ~

How do you access your within?

Do you journey? Do you close your eyes and visit an inner room? Do you ask or pray or seek or don a veil? Do you chant, meditate and clear your mind?

What if it was possible to get in so that you could get down into what really mattered? They say that the brain, when it enters into the state of wonder through inquiry, is able to expand into the cosmic territory of what hasn't happened yet, so instead of referencing the past, the almost future is available. How cool, right?

What if your Muse had her dwelling in that almost future space? What would you say when you saw her there?

Imagine you are bringing tea to your Muse and you can ask any question you want. First, see yourself handing her the tea, and she sips . . . then you ask your question . . . then she speaks . . . what does she say?

Lick the Fire

You don't have to trust the process.
You just have to keep moving forward
through the fear.

If we had certainty,
if we could control the outcome,
the risk wouldn't be there
and without the risk
the growth does not run deep.

Believe me, it would
not be nearly as fun, or
transformative.

I try not to promise trust, or safety.
Art is not safe at all.
This is what you can trust:
It will take you into
dangerous territory, but,
you won't be harmed.

Honor your instincts
instead of your controlling nature.
Stop trying to understand,
to grasp, to know, to get the
hang of it. Really, stop it.

The true work will often
feel like you are about
to lift off, to fly.
Feels like bliss and
throwing up all at once.

Enjoy the uncertainty of the ride.
Stop trying to predict or
create the outcome.
Stop convincing yourself
you have to trust and be fearless.
You don't.

There is a new story,
the only storyline is this one:
KEEP DOING IT.
That's it. That is how you
will get where you need to go.

Stop requiring so much
security during your process.
Let the free fall be your lover,
the feeling of 'no bottom' be welcome.

Welcome the thought:
you might not get this one right.
Welcome the Uh-Oh! at the
beginning of almost
every possibility.

Release the need to dominate.
Submit.
Let the process make
you come completely undone.

Drop your ribbons
to the floor and laugh
and cry and lay your
head upon your creation.

Keep the dialogue happening,
say it out loud.
Talk to the muse as if
she could really hear you. She can.

By allowing the fear to
be there without stopping
your work, the chatter
will not cease, but it will change.
You are the over-comer now.

You are an unstoppable creative.
You don't have to trust the process.
Just don't put your brush, pen or drum down.
Don't put it down. Listen. Allow yourself
to get scared to life instead of scared to death.

Don't step back from the flame.
Lick the fire. Be burned if you have to.
Put the ashes into the creation.
All of it, every fear and wound,
becomes useful here.

Desire trumps the need to trust.
If you are not shaking in your boots
you haven't yet even arrived.

For my love, my husband Jonathan Lewis,
when he was still my fiancé

~ Radical Surrender ~

Where are you needing to take a big daring risk?

Are you being held back by your fear? Always hesitating even when you feel there is a song calling to your soul?

What would happen if you moved into those spaces without needing to trust? You might get hurt; it's true, it could happen, but are you willing to live from a space where you aren't risking? Are you willing to get hurt?

We are so fond of saying trust the process, but then we are seeking that feeling of 'trust' and if we don't feel it, because the process seems so wild and unpredictable, like art for example, we pull back. What if instead of pulling back, we moved forward?

Imagine there is an area of your life you haven't been willing to look at with truly open eyes. Perhaps it is fear that has been holding you back. What is that area? What does it look like in symbol or metaphor? Choose to see it now freshly, even with trembling. How does it feel and what does it make you want to do?

See if the Muse wants to show you anything about it, consider asking for a light…

Reorientation to the Universe

Here's how it works:
Be utterly fascinated.
Walk around in awe at
and with the universe.

Whisper unrealized dreams into the cosmos.
Imagine star shaped ears leaning in.
Hanging on your every word.
You matter.

Sometimes you have to step out of
what you know and visit other realms.
Creative beings are like that.
Always wondering around.

Here's what's real:
What's real is what you love.
Are you free enough to love what you truly love?
When you love what you love, life becomes real.

Real means we are not asleep anymore,
it doesn't mean reality is 'as it seems.'
Your willingness to step into this kind of realness
shows you where to look and with what kind of seeing.

Pause a moment with me,
just here, inside the spaciousness of this concept
and move yourself just off the gridlines
of your usual track and frame.

This shift might seem
almost imperceptible at first,
but it could be the quantum leap
in a much smaller package of potential.

This is more than a shift in perspective,
this is a re-orientation to the Universe itself
Will you dare to open new eyes
or open new ears?

To live here in the presence of Glory
isn't something for the special people.
It is for those who are willing to participate
in it, wonderstruck drunk with beauty.

What would I tell you
if I could tell you anything?
You can participate in the life of the Beloved.
You are a part of the Beloved itself.

I want you to hear this:
You are a part of everything.
This is the most important theory of all.
Enter this field of being through awareness.

Try this.
Speak and sing into water before sipping or dipping.
Walk the earth as sacred ground. Listen to the trees.
Understand this. You are standing in the cosmos.

If you walk around like this you are sure
to fall in love with the theory of everything.

Try this. *Be utterly fascinated*
with each other and with everything.

We live between two worlds
and if you can keep one
foot in each, you will learn to dance
in new and exciting ways!

Listen to this.
None of this is about
keeping up or getting it right,
free yourself from concepts of rightness.

We are cultivating our own cultures
that make us giggle and and gasp and
lead to experiences filled with utter enthrallment
Awe even.

Drop to your knees in
praise and gratitude
at the awareness that any
of this exists in the first place.

The willingness to accept
you have relevance in the unfolding of the
Great Mystery will do you more good
than you can possibly imagine.

Whatever this is really is,
you belong here and have goodness to share.
And besides all that,
I like being here, with you.

~ New Framework ~

What is the framework you are operating within?

A framework is how you see the world, view the universe and yourself in it. Often we don't choose it; it gets stuck on a default setting from the time we are young.

Your framework is like a pair of glasses shaped from childhood that we used to help us see, but now we have outgrown them; they don't fit our face, our life, or our way of seeing, but we keep looking because we don't know there is another way. This could be called your outlook or world view, or perspective. This is back to the old, glass half full or empty, but it is deeper and more dangerous than that because it shapes every choice you make. For some reason, we have to fit it into our framework; or if it is beyond the edges of what we can see in the frame, it threatens our identity and we want to cut it out and stay safe.

Imagine you are given a new pair of glasses with an entirely new framework. What do the glasses look like? And do they have special powers? What do they help you see that you weren't seeing before? If your Muse gave them to you – do they have special powers?

The Day Will Come

The day will come
when you are sitting
having your tea
you will look back
at the not so distant past
and wonder
why you didn't pick up
your paintbrush,
why you didn't write
that novel,
why you didn't risk
being a fool for love.

The day will come
when you are sitting
having your tea
and you will cry over the ways
you were mean and hard
when you could have
been soft and loving,
when you chose reason
over possibility and regretted it
when you chose the wrong
person one more time.

The day will come
when you are sitting
having your tea
you will choose not to wait anymore
for anything to change

in order to say, "Yes,"
when you choose yourself
as your own great work in the world.
When you feel in your bones
that even if you didn't
do most of the things you
thought you wanted to
and it didn't turn out the way
you hoped
You can choose aliveness
as your path
and only look back
when it serves you.

Choose your life
as the great adventure
that is happening right now.
Be amazed at the legend that
has become your very own life.

The day will come
when you are sitting
having your tea
and will smile into your cup
and in your heart
you will find tenderness for yourself
and others.
Despite the challenges
you have faced and will face,
you can call it:
good. GOOD.
This will be a good day.

For Bing

~ Taking Action ~

What must you absolutely do in order to feel fulfilled?

What if your life was run by your regrets instead of your desires? That would feel terrible wouldn't it? Most of us would agree, and yet many of us are living from that space, allowing what we didn't do to inform what we are doing. Now that has to end, today.

Take a moment to look back at your life to the things and people and opportunities that you said no to that you wish you had said yes to. Dream on how your life might be different if you didn't have the story of the one that got away, whether that is a person, an opportunity, a way that you hurt someone, a regret.

Imagine that your future was regret free, and that you continued to choose things that were in alignment with the language your soul speaks. What would that look like? Choose to see at least two situations, potentials in which your soul is asking you to show up.

Give this regret free feeling to your Muse – and have her show you the freedom that is possible. This may be a good time to dance…. dancing the future into being….

Cages of Our Own Making

I let myself out of my cage.
I saw the door
for the first time
and I just stepped out.
It was so easy!
It's so beautiful out here!
Surprised at my sudden freedom
I looked back
to see that open door
and the structure in
which it was housed.
But it was already gone.
Stunned, I wondered,
was it me the whole time?
Nobody put me there,
no jailer but my own self?
Ha! I wanted to cry
but instead I started laughing.
In that laughing
I remembered what I forgot
so long ago: Who I am.
Let the dancing begin!

~ Releasing Yourself ~

Where can you release yourself from self-imposed bonds?

Is there a particular wound, bound up in your story, that is ready to be let go of? Is there something, some hurt, you are allowing to run the show instead of some LOVE that would like to be in charge?

What if it is truly as simple as choosing to step out from under that tyranny. Would you be willing? Quiet as it's kept, we also get something out of our cages. Sure, they keep us safe, but there is something else. Sometimes that something else is making someone else wrong from the vantage point of our self-imposed cage that keeps everyone else out and us in.

Imagine the cage that is coming to mind as you read this. See it, for what it is. Give language to it. Call it by name. See what or who it is made of. The colors, textures, words and the door that opens it. Is there a key? Call it out.

Then. Step out. Yes. Just step out. See the cage dissolve and then see yourself walking or flying away. . . .

Unfettered: A Rant for Overcoming

Release me from beneath your gaze,
your view of me, and your ways.
I am coming out from underneath
the layers of consciousness, not mine,
those I have taken on without my choice,
and those I took on by choice too,
I release you.

I don't want your concept of fear
of what will happen if I do this or that,
or *don't* do this or that just the right way
to create a desired outcome in this
world or the next. I am not here
to gain or earn a reward, but to live fully now,
and in living, express my gifts freely
without apology or fear of repercussion.
Though I know repercussion always comes.

I don't want to be in fear that
blessings only come to those that think
and act in this particular way each day.
Or call on this concept or that one
inside of this system or another.
I don't accept your definition of beauty
or success or right living or wrong living,
for that matter.
These definitions are trappings unwelcome.

No, I am not a victim.
I have chosen willingly, but now also choose
to let them go.

I don't know very much.
But I know this: Everyone here is on a journey
and we have no idea whatsoever
about this road we are on
speculating about
why things aren't going well
for us and why it is like this
is just another made
up belief system in an effort to make sense
of the madness and make ourselves feel better.
Admit it. You don't know why, in any real
sense, why she died of cancer or why he
had a stroke. There is really no way to know.
Strangely or not so strangely we long for reason which
can only be explained as unreasonable.

What of the mystery, my friends?
What happens if we surrender our need to know,
or better yet, a need to be right about anything
at all? If you don't want
to acknowledge there is madness,
then we have very little to talk about.

Yes, I am shaking my beliefs free.
I am letting go of the impact
of positive thinking on the psyche
of the soul that just needs to mourn
however she needs to mourn,

in whatever way, for however long.
No one needs to interpret that
for her. She needs no interpreter.
Only the sacred spaciousness is
needed to unfold herself as she sees fit.

I don't want to be defined by
Mercury retrograde, what is in
my seventh house and where I am
in my hurdle through space
and time towards womanhood
or where I should or shouldn't
be by the age of 43, or when
gray hairs come for you or me.

I particularly don't want to live behind
a concept of keeping up –
That one just bores my Muse and me
and drives us to inactivity.

I am sick and tired of the ones I serve
who are sick of fearing the condemnation
of the positive thinking brigade.
What a relief to them, when I tell them:
This tragedy might have nothing to do with you
or karma or your childhood or your thoughts.
This might just be chaos and crossfire.
Wide-eyed, they lay their burden down
and proceed with the work of healing
without the shame of personal causation
or persecution from an invisible god.
This does not change the power of

good thoughts on our challenges.
But every tragedy is not self-induced.
This is a lie. Stop telling it. It was sold to our people.

I shall think my own thoughts.
Or at least attempt to.
Here I go:
I choose not to live in any fear.
There I said it out loud. *Did you hear me?*
I don't know how to do that
but I ask this now of my soul and body:
Lead me to the path unfettered
So I might walk freely upon this earth.
Knowing the nature of what is fallen here,
does not keep me from reveling in the
majesty of this creation called home.

I am untying the ribbons that
have bound me, silk ones and
chain-linked ones. Taboos are falling
from my ankles as I pace
new paths in the floorboards
through the pressure of poetry
pressing through me.

I write this for me, from me
but I hear the voices of many behind
and beside me acknowledging
this desire together: *a soul unfettered.*

Lift me up. Don't weigh me down.
I will do the same for you.

Let us move away from seeking
approval and into authentic expression.
Authentic expression can set us
free from the need to be seen
by others because we finally see ourselves.
I choose not to live *through* fear.
Though I know fear is a present teacher.
Jesus said perfect love casts out fear.
What is perfect love that I may cast
fear out from me? Or at least choose
to live from the space of the perfect love
He has for me. His love isn't based on
my performance or yours. This is not
a performance at all. This life is a learning
of how to lean into the great big love
of ever-present-ness despite our selfishness.

I choose to live beyond cause and effect,
there is so much more going on here.
I do not want to protect myself in case
of disaster or attack because I don't
like the way it makes my mind work.
And no, I don't think my fear of it or denial
of it creates more or less bad things
happening.

The Blessed Mother also knows
there are riddles afoot in these hills.
The Universe does respond to me,
it is true, if I gaze at the electron
it also gazes at me, but it does
not bring me harm if I fear harm

or bring me harm to teach me a lesson.
Whatever thought that needs
to come up with my tea - we can
set the record straight and liberate
a belief from its cage.

I am writing this because
I want to walk fearlessly.
Not because I am not in awe of God,*
(Did you know, in the Bible,
the word fear is often translated as Awe,
Reverence and Amazement?)

Grace is either grace or it isn't.
And yes, grace is amazing.
You cannot earn it, it is freely
given and it is ever-present and
all we need to do is allow
ourselves to enter into it.
It is not a reward.
For this I send up a shout of praise
to the Most High.
And what about Faith?
Faith isn't something that
comes because everything goes
as you hoped,
but something that is created
because it doesn't
go as you hoped, and still
you don't lose your mind
and the crack in your heart lets the
light in and breaks you open.

But really I have no idea what
faith is. I still choose to surround
myself with it like a garment,
having no idea what it is
and I am not required to know.

Don't take on anything here
that doesn't serve you. I am
neither teacher nor guide,
but fellow traveler here on earth.
A poet perhaps.
I am not someone who thinks
I belong somewhere else.
I am from this earth and this is my home.
I refuse to feel displaced
and fear the life to come if
we do this or don't do that.
I can love this earth and work for
her wellness without needing
fear of her ending, or of mine,
as motivation. I love because I love,
not because fear of what will
happen motivates me to action.
I am motivated through unreasonable
love for my fellow travelers.

This is my rant for overcoming
over-culture, inner-culture, and under-culture.
An attempt through writing
to get free of these proverbial
ties that bind. I am not calling
for a new belief to settle in

or a change to finally come
or a new declaration to live by.

I am calling for a cycle:
no belief system to define and confine
my restless heart. That's just it.
My heart wants to roam free.
I just want to experience
being free from ideas
of being or not being.
I want to feel unfettered.
And. I do.

For Siddha Light and Karuna

~ Deep Listening ~

What is your soul trying to communicate to you?

Our soul is always trying to get us to listen. When we don't it may go dormant for a while, or seem to, but it will emerge and it might not be as gentle the next time, as your soul will use any means necessary to get your attention, to get you to wake the f*ck up from your slumber.

The waking up may involve a setting oneself free from the previous ties that bind, a letting go of old ideas and selves and relationships.

Imagine that your soul was speaking directly to you and asking you to untie some old things you don't need anymore. See the knots. See them being released. Let go. Be free, darling one. Be free. Any knots you don't need anymore are dissolving.…

Medicine Woman

The wild one lives within all women.
She is known as Medicine Woman.
She holds tools for healing
in her magic basket.
She sings her prayers.
Medicine Woman knows stars and sums.
She listens between worlds.
Medicine Woman cannot be domesticated,
at all, ever.
Even when we don't recognize her,
she is always here.
She has blue butterflies and red roses in her hair
and golden boots with wings.
She is at the movies
with teenage girls on Friday night.
She gets a tattoo of the Guadalupe
on her left bicep in San Francisco's Mission District
and the sacred heart of Jesus on her right bicep.
You may catch a glimpse
of her silver, striped leggings
as she roller skates through New York's Central park.
She teaches workshops on right-brain, left-brain,
the critic and her lover, the Muse
or the geometry of numbers
or raw food or
revolution for breakfast.
She pays for everything with cash.
She paints glitter on her toe-nails.
Fire Engine Red.

Just don't think you have her figured out.
She will always surprise you.
She shows up in a crimson dress
sewn with a white dogwood bodice
and bay leaf hem.
She is the sound of bells.
She may let her armpit hair grow.
She is the place within us that wants it all.
And wants to give it all up.
She swims naked in the ocean.
She rides motorcycles up the coast.
She paints, writes, dances, dreams,
and has multiple income streams.
She is medicine woman.
She heals the unexpressed in us.
She asks the question - *Who are you not being?*
Her life is her own. She is on her own.
And she likes it that way.
And don't be surprised if she asks you
to miracle tea and you find yourself
drunk with aliveness and honeycomb cake.

For my cousin, Bridget McBride

~ Your Medicine ~

What medicine do you carry within you?

Every one of has special medicine, our own mojo. Some of us cultivate it and share it out in the open. Others of us practice our quiet magic alone or in small circles. This medicine may be a gift, or a talent, or a way of accessing information or seeing. YOU do have some – and knowing what it is helps you tune into a greater revelation of ourselves.

Imagine that you are a medicine woman - what do you carry in your medicine basket? Pretend like you can see what is in there and that you know what it is for. One by one pull things out of it and see if you can find out what each one represents!

This is a fun practice to hand over to your muse, and allow yourself to be surprised. Consider drawing some of the items in the basket. Ask the items what they are for.

Muses and Men ~ A Transition

Dear One,

This is a page for breathing
representing a transition.
Ah. Thank you.

The Muse has spoken to the collective.
To our dreams, ideas & desires.
Now it gets personal.
Some say nothing is personal.
Or that everything is personal.
This part is also about my muse.
My personal muse.
And about men. And loss.
Most of the writings in Part One were
in the feminine or to women, mostly.
Not because I don't love men, but
because I write for women.
Now a few 'menz' coming in.
My dad for one.
My first lost marriage.
Spiked with a few lovers for flavor.
Add family, a dike, and some mermaids.
Stir.
Then, the revelation of new love.
A love I didn't believe would happen.
But it did and I am happy to share those with you
to lighten the load of the heavier writings.

For this section the Muse invites you to something harder if you happen to
still drink. A glass of wine, a whiskey, a martini with two olives please,
for me. Shaken hard. And Up.

Part Two

Fuse

MY RESTLESS MUSE
Having Her Way With Me

holds the prayers of the World

Dear Reader,

I called this book Tea with the Midnight Muse based on my inner wild world. But until recently I cut a lot of the ones in this collection out. They felt too personal to share. I only just recently put them back in when I was almost done with the entire editing process. I thought, how can this book be called Tea with the Midnight Muse if you take out the juicy, dark, tangled bits and leave them only light to weave with?

Perhaps learning more about my Muse, and my dark side correlated with her and how she has her way with me, will be an entry into your own Muse relationship. In this book I have tried to provide encouragement: the poem opens your mind, the inquiry makes it personal to you, and the teaching helps you shift it and ground, and then imagination takes you on a personal journey into how to make any of this useful – how to cause a transformation with imagination as your guide.

I hope that through connecting with the wily ways of my own Muse, something in yours will stir. I will allow the dark underbelly of my creativity to be shared with you and trust you will still love me in the morning. They are perhaps the most important ones for me personally and creatively, and deserve their own book but alas, they asked to be included. That Muse.

To introduce and provide some context for this section I am including a recent writing, inspired by the question, Where I Come From, inspired by a process led by George Ella Lyon, the Poet Laureate of Kentucky

Signed in red butterflies,
Shiloh Sophia

Where I'm From

I am from cinnamon toast and honey milk,
and from warm beds with more than enough pillows.
I am from enough time for me
with enough time for you.
I'm from the land of women.
I am from the heart of my mother's love
and breastfeeding.
I'm from the colored fabric swatches
of my mother's mother.
From the incense, icons and candles
of my father's mother
I'm from my father's unlived stories
of true love.

I am from the good witches
on the wrong side of the tracks,
from tarot cards, tai chi, spells,
lesbians and wild redheads.
I'm from scriptured women
who go thump with the Bible
who find their tables filled
with friends in need of prayer.

I'm from days of prophecy pie
and fear of the Lord
laced with fear of not becoming
the fully unfettered me.
I'm from baked beans with Best Foods mayo
in ceramic bowls,

and from patchwork dresses
and roast chickens with Sue sauce.

I am from Elvis records
and hot pink curlers in blonde hairs.
I'm from the longing and the howling at the moon.
I'm from red roses in bowls of water blessings
and from quantum physics for breakfast.

I am from two women. A poet and a painter.
Precise. Pottery. Prophesy. Paradox. Wet paint.
I am from the one who thins her own forest
with a chainsaw,
and from the one who is in love with language.
The first word they taught me was 'moon'

I am from dust,
from in the beginning was the Word
and the spit of Christ mixed with the soil of seeing.
I am from the particles of a love pure enough
to raise the dead
and put peace in the heart of my chaos.

I am from the non-judgement of transvestites
in red dresses and high heels on Sunday morning in San Francisco's
Glide Gospel streets.
I am from learning to love the Lord
from African Americans
who took me under their wings
into the streets of creation.

I am from Native Americans
who showed me where I live
smudged me from childhood
and would not let me forget.
I am from the United States,
occupied territory, red.
My teachers have called me to action, Aho!

I am from my sister the Cinnamon Cowgirl,
a bad ass on a motorcycle
with a devil-may-or-may-not care
blues song blazing.
I am from my brother the carpenter
hammering out
an uncertain future with
many daughters to call his own.

I am from my sister in the deserts of Mexico
with her miracle child holding the family secrets.
I am from the Virgin de Guadalupe's crescent moon
and from making wrong things right.

I am from willing to die for love dreams
and from ten years of prayers and miscarriages.
I am from matriarchs and yet finally choose:
I will not walk the path of the Matriarch.

I am from the Northern parts of California
from more homes than I can count
from rolling green hills
and grey blue beaches and seagulls that love pepperoni pizza

I am from the walk on the wild side
with a Prince tattoo
from his 1982 love symbol.

I'm from the constellation called Cosmic Cowgirls
and my imaginary white horse is named Commander
which has now become a reindeer from the North.

I am from the need to gather the women,
the mending power of circle and drum and feather.
I am from ancient Russian women
grandmother shamans
and Scandinavian grandfathers
who hollowed musical instruments out of myrtle wood.

I am from the kitchen of the Red Madonna
Mother of the all seeing all forgiving
One whose enormous tent stretches from star to star.
I am from Her mothership and from His Gospel.
I am from legends. I am from freedom.
I was born for hot summer days with nowhere to go
with my West Virginia lover in a white convertible.
I am made from adventure, that is my middle name now.

I am forged from the riddle bone of my Muse
who loves leopard print and ghetto saloons
eats chocolate with peanut butter by candlelight,
she writes poetry from a red chair at midnight.

I am from the colors of woman
from a sisterhood
who seek to serve to transform

wounds into wonders
through the alchemy of dancing paintbrushes.

I am from mermaids in monster trucks
Who do sing to each to each
who tell tall green tales to salty sailors
seducing them with martinis, two olives please.
I am flown from wonder woman in her glass plane.

I am pulled from stardust into matter,
I am star woman.
I am pulled to the gravity of earth,
I am earth woman.
I am from the need for justice for all
and all kinds of kindnesses.

I am from falling in love with each day like a school girl crush.
I am from the mother tongue of creativity
expressed with intentionality
I'm from the impossibility.
I'm from being totally for you without losing me.
I am from the mystics of the red thread café
a place between tomorrow and today,
I'll meet you there.
Where the mysteries of the universe
drop colored ribbons like clues
just on the other side of the narrow gate.

Fiddle of Light

make me a fiddle made of light
strung in silken chord
a bone hollowed out
so it will hum and ring
adorn the body of my fiddle
with red butterflies.
red to remind me of the scar
that you pulled the fiddle from.
along the ragged edge
you dragged your holy blade
to take material for my fiddle
and cleaned up the opening
with your own tears.
not unlike adam's own rib
the fiddle is, the rib of me, whittled down
and weightless like light.
in the wake of that cut,
there were thousands of tiny
itsy, bitsy, chrysalis that clung
to the edge unborn and shimmering
see them glimmering in the full moon?
when I play my fiddle that you made
the butterflies can lift out one wet wing
and then another and fly around
as long as they come back to me
so I don't forget who I am.
I need my fiddle to be waterproof
otherwise I fear the hot salty sorrow
will melt it down.

teach me how to play it
to give levity to my gravity
and cause my bare feet to jig again.
teach me to sing the song again
or a new one, if you have a spare.
make my fiddle la mariposa roja
so that in its bright company
I might begin to fly with
wings clipped. heal. heal. heal.
I trust in the song of a fiddle
made this way, composed
of soul and scar blood
and butterfly wisdom
It is in these sacred things
that I can learn to trust
the song of the universe again
and find that a red key
has been placed on
a red thread tied to my belt
so that as I dance
It hits my thigh and reminds
me of sacred things
like following the smell
of cinnamon rolls to my
mother's kitchen at sunrise.
like sitting at tea with
women who run with wolves
and knowing how to speak in stars.
like taking kisses from
unassuming almost lovers
to test their salt and sweet

before consumption.
like putting my moon blood
onto my fingertips
before I play the next song.

Soul Calligraphy

Today,
poetry called me home
through open doors

I ran,
seeking shelter
a hiding place
I followed the hum in the floorboards
laid by the ancestors
until I found the darkest closet
that was waiting for my name
to be written inside

The first act I committed
was to paint calligraphy
on all the white walls
so that I could be covered in language
I could not see anything
but the brush in my hand
knew the shape of my soul letters
and obediently used the blood
from the carcass I carry
for the ink

I have carried this wounded animal
with me everywhere,
dead so long but still warm
and non-decomposing
like the bodies of the saints

I lift the carcass
from each doorway
where it tries to lay its
tired bones down to die
but I keep rousing it and dragging it along with me
and it is no surprise to find
it here with me in the closet of myself

I lift the effigy of it up like a holy thing
that I could not stop worshipping
Crouched in my closet
I could hear all of you
in yours, murmuring
your chants and whistles
and clucking for your own
language to find its way
to your pen

So many instruments in this house
for wayward poets

Though the bombings
continued around us
we could hear the slaughter
of the innocents
rage on and on
we spread our palms
on the threshing floors
and listened through our hands
to the stories yet to be told
and the stories told already

We listened with ears rubbed
raw from the salt of tears

And so this is how it ends
I lay my body down stretching
from one end to the other
and curling my toes up the wall
to make myself fit

So this is how it ends
I fold my arms across my chest
Expecting to die.
A thought rises

So this is how it begins
It is time to make
coconut curry soup
for the guests who are coming.
Though I do not know
who they are

This place has called them
to be harbored up here
with us
and how nice it would be
if they could smell the soup
from the road
through the smoke and mirrors
we use to keep
real strangers out

I rise now
with only the hope
of coconut milk to guide me

I open the door
and walk into the light
And this time forget
to drag the carcass
because I am thinking
of digging up onions
from the back yard
for the soup
And I wonder,
Is this what healing is?

To forget a little at a time
that which hurts
while remembering
that which blesses?

I join the others who
are taking turns
chanting lines of poetry
over the soup
I have made.

Hungry Muse

My Muse is hungry.
Feed her chocolate and red beer.
Give her purple lingerie
trimmed in lavender lace.
Give her quills with gold ink
for goodness sakes.
Don't you know what's at stake?

My Muse is hungry
So please give her freckled shoulders to kiss.
Please, oh please no guilt sandwiches
shall be served at the Red Thread Café.
Give her cheeseburgers with extra mayo
and don't hold the bread and whatever you
do . . . please, please take her out to the beach
in a shiny red convertible.
She needs to wear
rhinestone sunglasses and collect
stones for the altar.

My Muse is hungry
So, share with her, oysters and champagne
but whatever you do
do not wait too long between kisses.
My Muse is hungry
So, always know that foie gras
and poetry will suffice on any
Monday night.
Please know that singing songs by

moonlight and dancing in
parking lots drunk with hope
is something that will make her
do . . . almost anything.

My Muse is hungry
for more than bucket lists
her appetite cannot be satiated with
interesting, small or even big talk.
She needs insight for breakfast.
Revolution for lunch.
Salsa and cowboy boots for dinner,
and infinite options for playing.
Yes, playing. Muses, you see . . .
can get fed up with the mediocrity
of the moment. Sad but true. They
are restless creatures.
They need more than most,
and give more than most.
YES, they are ever so difficult and radiant
and they want to have the keys to
every door that needs opening.
If you want to be awake in this world.
instead of sleep-walking along
these messy streets of existence
then whatever you do:
don't take your Muse for granted
or you might find yourself
hungry for something
that nothing at all will ever fill.
And you might wonder,
where or where has my little Muse gone?
Oh where, oh where can she be?

Love's Kitchen and the Ghetto Muse

My Muse prefers to live in the hood
under the hood of old red trucks
Inside the wink of the hoodwinked story
The hood of my upper lid winking
The hood gathering grease from the fried chicken
The hood way out on the edge of town
where she lifts her outskirts
while she dances in the dusty streets
past the tracks on the wrong side of town.
What is it about her that seeks
tattoos with barbed wire and fire hearts?
What is it about her that likes the smell
of the stranger's sweat because it is so personal?
Why must she insist on playing ukulele barefoot
like a wayward waif at train stations?
Her jar, instead of saying TIPS
says, "Take One" and it is filled with dollar bills.
By the end of the day,
there is so much money
she calls a feast of Muses
and in they all come,
Bejeweled and bold
they pour into love's kitchen.
you can find her,
most days digging up bones
from the cracks in the sidewalk,
pimpin' sunglasses with rhinestones
and no bra and if you didn't know
better you might mistake her

for someone you used to know
that you forgot long ago
and are happy to see.
Love's kitchen is past the old,
abandoned house
with the windows boarded up;
past the new side of town
where no one keeps their
curtains open
just past the county jail
where many of her cousins
write poetry on concrete walls
just past the Guadalupe shrine
where the thousands who
have lost their lives are
sung to by their sisters
and brothers while lighting
candles to every
Nuestra Señora of something.
You will be able to smell
the fried chicken cooking
when you get close
Don't forget to bring
a rose or a bar of chocolate
and a paintbrush.
Love's kitchen doesn't
open until midnight.
We are saving a seat for you and your true love at the bar

This Terrible Longing

This terrible longing which has no end
has me sniffing the trails of wolves
and following them where I ought not go.
I am a jar broken that carried all
the lightning bugs of love in the world.
Crash! Out they came one night
with unbearable beauty.
Then they flew off to light on the lure
of some other new lovers.
I got called down, down
to the place where pomegranates are eaten
in the dark while whispering the fugue
in between red drops consumed.
If you do not wish to visit with me there tonight,
then go on home and make yourself some tea.
Pull the covers up to your chin,
but don't blame me
if you keep reading and wish you hadn't.
My joy was swallowed by those lightning bugs
now flown off, for careless consumption by lovers
lounging on blankets in the afternoon sun
eating mangos of timelessness.
I wish those young lovers well
and hope they never read this.
We used to be those young lovers.
Now I bite my lips dry without the kisses
I had learned to live on like food.
I am not ashamed to call myself a fool for love.

I am proof that true love can exist
where danger lives.
I am proof that love between humans
does not conquer all, after all.
Was it something else all together?
Was it something else that interfered
in the woven togetherness of vows forged?
The vessel of my union was sealed –
sealed with love, protection, and passion.
and yet fear encased my heart
and I was tangled in a chain of love with no key.
I chose those links myself and let them dig into
my flesh. I wore them like dark jewelry
because of love; true, terrible, and oh, quite real.
The lightning bugs lit everything up anyway
and made me bracelets of light to see by
and protect me like Wonder Woman.
How did anything get past our garden gates?
Where was that opening? I think I know, but
I don't want to say it out loud. Suffice it to say
white man's under-the-counter-magic-meds
are not the way to heal a broken limb of self.
It opens doors that are meant to stay shut.
I lived with the muck of the devil's tracks
on my kitchen floor. I would wipe them up
each morning and look out my kitchen window
hopeful anyway.
I had 'happy' in my every single day
when I speak of it, women find this hard to believe.
Men look in wonder, but seem to understand more
of how hardness and softness co-exist.

I called him tricky then, the devil that is.
Now I don't call him anything because he
doesn't live at my house anymore.
He lost his name on my doorstep,
when you walked out the door.

For Rahm Isaiah

Grafting the Burning Bush

Come with me
for the story of
a sudden expansion of my heart.
I can feel the pulsation of me
Pushing, pulling, straining at the chains
to break them into pieces
the little swords pushing out,
clinking to the floor.
The scars are stretching
against their constraints
this sudden expansion of territory.
The supernova of this encounter
humbles me. This is sacred ground.
I bow to the greatness,
to the awe I feel.
I bow with my head pressed in prayer
with scriptures at my fingers.
I feel the word of God inside me now.

As you pass through hell
with your hair on fire,
don't forget to hum the tune
to Gloryland so you can find your
way through the caves
that echo:
the future is unwritten.

Healing is mine now and I dance.
At the easel, I paint the hearts
of fire and pray God to listen

to the prayer which will not
leave my lips.

I will not go to sleep on the questions love asks.

This inquiry into the quiet space between us
is expanded by the breath of God.
Breathe God with me, Breathe God with me.
Breathe God with me, Breathe God with me.
Press the scars of you into my tender places,
until we no longer care where the scars came from
because God is grafting the burning bush into wisdom.

God's own heart beats inside of all of us.
Wounds to wisdom, hear me roar.
Last night I swallowed the burning bush
and I dreamed it became my very own heart.
Our scars became the crossroads
where Jesus rose to life in the garden.
He handed us both a rose, with thorns.
He greeted us with open wounded palms
and told us, "*Come unto me,*"
and he said: *coming unto me is*
coming unto one another

I think I understand. Yanked by the hair,
I noticed all the light coming from the scar,
the light from the wound
that lights up the cosmic city of humanity.
You who serve me and through me, serve Him
and I serve the Red Madonna
who rises in my heart, a red star of ragged hope, rises.

Mother Tongue

Poetry came and took me
by the scruff of my neck
and dragged me across the
flames of my old stories.

I cried out ~
Let me be!
I have work
to do
that is not this.

Poetry would not listen.
With its words in edgewise
teeth biting into
the underbelly.

I cried out
I did not think you:
Poetry of all the Muses, would
be so cruel, so violent.

Poetry stared me down,
unmoved by my protests.

The white bones of poetry
were poking me in the ribs,
while someone was
in the kitchen making sizzling
fried chickens and singing a jig.

I cried out ~ Enough!
Too much!
Must everything come into me at once?
Is this what all poets must endure?

I'll do it.

I found myself standing
at the very sharp edge
of a blank page,
located in a book as large
and lovely as a church.

Wait, there were a few words,
don't miss the fine print.
It read:
Your life starts here.
It was in my own handwriting.
I got on my hands and knees
kneeled onto the page.
and I drew the pen
as a warrior
draws the sword.

The first words I wrote scribed in
the new book of myself:

Mother Tongue.

MOTHER TONGUE
Born This Way

CHAPTER 9

Dear Reader,

I am the child of three parents. I am so very much a part of each of them, it makes me laugh! They imparted their essence to me through teachings, conversation, art work and just through their love of me.

Each one is a mystic of a certain kind - all are rebels in their own minds. I am a braid of their lives and loves and eccentricities. In many ways all three were free in their thinking, even if their lives were caught up in being.

The section ends with poems I wrote about myself, that resulted from the parents they are. We aren't any kind of normal family, but I am ever so grateful to have been called in by these three, Greg, Caron and Sue. Lucky me,

Signed in White Lightening,
Shiloh Sophia

p.s. White lightening was the name. Explains a lot doesn't it if one chooses when and how they show up.

My Father's Hair is Summer Grass

The smell of summer grass
always makes me think of my father.
That first summer I spent
with him when before my moon
and before any of us were too broken.

I longed to wrap my arms around his waist
when he rode his motorcycle
up and down those gravel roads,
taking turns too fast so I would
have to hold on tight. It was
before helmets, so I let his long
hair fly into my face and I could
smell the summer grass.

And now as I grow older,
I can see that his nose is my nose
and his forearms are also mine
and his mystical self, so much
the wild child and scholar,
has been passed to me.

Without so much of a,
"Hey here you go kid,"
or a warning that his
nature would be imparted to me in restlessness.
One day I told his mother
that I would rather perch atop a hill
and hunker down through the years

than work in white man's world again.
She said, "Just like your father."
I did not know then he was a mystic gone wrong.

For Gregory Scott Davis

A Stroke Called Hoya

I am this brush
that belongs to the Master
who lives down in the valley
I rise with her each day
and sleep by her side each night
and marvel at the strokes
she makes in cosmic light.

I am this brush
that knows the way to the
deep places in the wood
and the underside of stones
and the symphony of the moss
and brings home all of this
onto the canvas of her cosmos

I am this brush,
not that brush or her brush
or his brush.
I am THIS brush
that belongs to the woman
who has shown the path to many
and so with generosity,
I do offer myself back to her
how she searches through
the DNA molecules for how
together we can create
moments of arrival from
the cosmos to earth.

Form cometh forth from me.
See how this goes?

This brush which creates
angels. owls. horses.
mothers and children.
apple trees.
cells that divide and are so lovely
they look like a heart
that has never been hurt before.

There are places between places
and spaces between spaces
where the stars poke through
in cinnamon-colored light.
This is the place you will find this brush,
gathering particles of encodings
and information as I go,
so that when she lifts me
from my clay vessel for the day
I have done the work worthy
of a brush stroke
called Hoya.

For Sue Hoya

Death and the Intimacy of the Laundry

death doesn't enter as a destroyer
death enters in waves of intimacy.
today i am washing clothes still damp from death,
i can smell last breaths on every fiber
the overalls covered in paint and leaves
tender moss clinging to my hands
the white shirt you wore to 'dress up'
to go to the museum. the black pants, rolled.
your Carhartt jacket and workpants
all jumbled up with towels used these last days.
i don't want the death clothes
to touch the living clothes.
i am trying to keep things separate
so i don't lose my place. this is all sacred work.

i unroll the pant legs gingerly and curiously
tiny tree bits fall to the
ground but a lizard would not surprise me my dear.
yes i know i will only have this one
chance to shake the mountain
from off of your clothes.
now it is my clothes that carry
the mountain and the scent of
wood smoke, rain and food cooked on the stove.
my dear teacher,
in this vigil of you and your heart
i haven't missed a beat. but I miss yours now.
with the searching eyes of the archeologist
i explore cadmium orange and thalo blue strokes

made upon a pant leg
once holding the thigh of the artist.

I shake them out of their intricately colored wad
and see if I notice which color
went with which painting, when.
your garments.
you have shaken off your garments
once and for all.
a snake from her skin you slid
smoothly and silently from me.
i watched as you moved beyond
the horizon, beyond what i could
ever see and know.
Leaving your cosmic address once and for all.
in one deft brush stroke
you moved from snake to bird and flew free of your gravity. whoosh.
each sock and black ribbed tank top i examine for stickers and burrs
we do this you know –
poets have tea with death
and the intimacy of laundry –
we wonder, is this the last burr of hers i
will ever have the chance to pull
from the burrow of the sock?
so it is precious.
it must all be done very mindfully.
even the discarded must be
done so with a thought towards
its usefulness. and what it meant to you.
i could write a poem of praise
for the usefulness of towels
during death at home

we brought you home.
we dressed you
in your painters smock from Paris
for the long bumpy ride up the mountain.
2.5 hours.
we just let go of all the tubes of ugliness
and could see your precious face
and we broke you out of that joint
after 7 days of your cosmic sleep.
we dared to free you from there and
we did.
Spirit Warrior spoke for all of us
with her drum and the ancestors sang.
i held your white tousled head
and listened for what wasn't being said.
and did speak to you clearly
and you did speak to me clearly,
from that other place you taught me about.
that is a story for another day.
so grateful were we, to bring you home.
carried down gravel rock
and road to a bed surrounded by your own art.
and cosmic lineage.
and us. you were surrounded by us.
we made it. alive. and yes, you seemed
much more peaceful here.
our friends came with chickens and beer
and chocolate and wore garments of
celebration instead of somber.
for 4 nights i lay beside you
and witnessed you move and breathe.
knowing each one, ragged and

smooth could be the last one.
i listened like a mother listens
to her baby sleep
each move witnessed,
you didn't wake again.
i learned to care for you and yes,
i was afraid of every fluid and
chortled gasp.

so so so grateful I am, for that week before
for all the laughing and
the complete peace between us. amen. amen. amen.
grateful for a lifetime of unconditional love given and received.
thank you.
your last breath came
while having tea at our usual time
with you.
my love and I reading to you
from your mentor guardian's books
about the sculptor within
and the stone that must weep.
when you no longer breathed I kept
reading and reading you a prayer of
sculptor's tools through my watershed of tears.

The nuns of Sacre Coeur from Paris covered you in hymns and hers.
we sang to you and washed you
with precious bay oil and tender heart oil from the
red headed women and bowls of water
with squash blossoms and roses.
we marked you with pure chalk from white egg shell
for purification, protection and cleansing (cascarilla)

we filled your spaceship with pine
as a tree of life spine running the whole
distance. layers upon layers of lavender, bay,
eucalyptus and Alice's lemon balm all around you
and yellow flowers around your head
a single fig leaf at your crown
a tiny bouquet of a rose from your garden from Mary.
a sign that spelled love and a heart made
of paintbrushes and clay face from long ago.
and, of course, your poem from my mother, Caron.
a red thread was placed in your hands
with that one paintbrush and carried
outside the box to our waiting hands.
from your hands to our hands.
they say those who are supposed to meet
are connected by an invisible red thread
since before birth. i believe.
we tied feathers to your red thread
and wrapped your box in a weaving.
raven. owl. woodpecker and turkey vulture.
many of us came to you and to me
and hundreds prayed through these days.
your spaceship was hand built from the
land and hand painted by many of us who love you.
we studied your images
and tried to make your signs
and coordinates on the spaceship
so 'all of you' could find your way home.
i struggled with star configurations
and arrows and dna helixes and patterns
that you know so well. encodings.
I didn't look in the clean clothes

for your final resting garment, although
I did consider it as being those famous striped overalls.
(those will be be framed) or auctioned at Sothebys for a mint

your final resting garment was
pure un-gessoed fine Irish linen
the color of new wheat.
you would have preferred we paint on it
but this decision was mine to make.
just that morning i prayed for a bolt of linen
only to walk into your bedroom
and find it there waiting
still in it's wrapper for a future
painting i will never get to see.
we swaddled you like a newborn welcoming you home.
thank you my cosmic heart.

Sue Hoya Sellars 1936-2014

Art as Antidote

You taught me that art was an antidote to violence.
Showed me how to turn the brush just so
as to send prayers to the women in need.
Showed me how to throw the pot with so much
love it could reach all the way to China.

When I was being knitted in the womb
you came and drew my mother's hands
knitting. You became my father taking
nothing from my Father but expanding
the matrix of care I would need.

You told me I was an artist, not
based on how well I did things,
you told me I was an artist despite
my complaints and resistance
to chop wood carry water mentoring.

You taught me café composed
of inquiry and imagination that
expands the mind and the heart.
You showed me how to see what
I wasn't seeing by looking where
I wasn't looking with eyes
I didn't know I had.

You gave me so much love
that you taught me what love
could feel like, be like, and should be

Always excited to see me,
you taught me gratitude in adversity.
The heart of femininity:
Strength. Insight. No apology.
Standing where no one else was standing.

You showed me this:
Van Gogh's sunflowers transform pollution.
Cassatt's happy babies fight child labor.
Beethoven's 'Ode to Joy' lifts depression.
Buckminster Fuller's roads prevent accidents.
Alice Walker's 'The Color Purple' raises awareness.
Rilke's young poet keeps us living the questions.
Klimt's kiss inspires us to seek that kind of embrace.
Rumi's reminder, "This is not a caravan of despair . ."
keeps us searching for the Beloved.
Chopin keeps us in deep listening wonder.
Georgia O'Keefe keeps us looking
far inside flower centers for what we aren't seeing.
Frida's painted stories invite us to dive into
the painful interiors and find the hidden stories.
Sue Hoya Sellars' angels remind us we
are more than we appear, stardust incarnate.
Our maestros of the spirit: the artists, the poets,
the composers of what is essential in life show us
that we are the antidote to ugliness and violence.
Maybe you don't believe me that art
is an essential thread in the fabric of the world.
I don't care if you believe me or not.
This is something I actually know. She taught me.

My Mother Notices Everything

My mother notices everything
The slick snail crossing the sidewalk
in front of us is her friend.
The morning has always been her ally
or so she made it seem.
She spared me the duty of things called chores
and instead sent me to my room
to memorize T.S.Elliot or Rilke
or study right angles at my drawing board.
My mother appreciates light.
angle. sound.
edge. fence post. ridge.
and circle curving softly
around every equation
and loves that the square knows
how to square even the circle.
She likes her pencils sharp
and her paintbrushes brushed
and her sock drawers color-coordinated.
I am my mother's daughter.
She showed me where to look.
I remember her most with
a tape measure over her shoulder and,
a pencil in her hand, wearing her glasses
as if visionary lenses peering at some
piece of fabric or flaming letter
God sent special delivery
because if there is anyone God likes to please
with his riddles, rhymes and prophecy,
I have no doubt that it is my Mother.

For Caron McCloud

The Gravity of Noticing

It has been told by my mama
that as a baby,
moon was my first word
when I saw the color pink
in a sunset, I became very excited
and began to jump up and down.

It has been told by my grandmother
that when I was just a tiny girl
before language, I would group quilting squares
into matching sets of colors
nodding and shaking my head
with my choices.

It has been told by the matriarch
that I was always an artist
and had the gift of seeing things differently
though sometimes I didn't believe it,
but finally I do.

Art has been in me all along.
And noticing.
Noticing that everything,
has a gravity to it
that links pain with beauty
that can sometimes be unbearable.
I cannot live without beauty.

Sometimes, I feel alone in my noticing.
(how vain)
I am struck dumb by a white bird on a hill.
Struck to tears by a spider spinning her web.
Struck to the core
by a man and woman dancing in a dusty bar.
Struck in the heart by texture
by color, by sound
by scent, by sight, by taste.

How do we fit it all in?
Where does it all go?
Into art. Into song. Into poetry.
How do we get all this living into our lives?

After crying into my beer
(Yes, I held it up to my eye)
What about us?
Those who notice everything,
and find ourselves heartbroken by beauty?
Whose lips do not cease to praise creation?
And stumble around in wonder?
When the heart aches,
we, in our isolation,
imagine ourselves to be
the only one crying in the world.
And so we reach out
to touch the tears of others
and remind ourselves
that we are not alone

in all this beauty
and all this suffering.
The gravity of noticing,
is a burden and a gift.
I am
this song of universe being sung.
I can only say;
thank you . . . thank you . . . thank you . . .
for these eyes.
This nose. This mouth.
This heart. This life.

Good Apple

My mother takes her place
beneath the branches of the tree of life.
She is sheltered there from sun and rain.
She nurtured me from the roots
she fed me from abundant fruits
she showed me the beauty in the blossom
she guided me to trace the bark with my fingers.
She taught me to stand with my back against this tree.
That I may be supported in the days of prophecy.
I am a grown woman now
who has taken my own place here
sheltered by the branches of the tree.
The prettiest one, my mother gave to me, apple.
I stand here beside my mother; see, I am near.
Green gold light patterning on our faces, dappled.
We look back through the garden gate wistfully
wondering when us sinners will be allowed to return
with our first mother, Eve, to our rightful places.

My mother, she told me something the other day.
She said when she lays down to sleep
she lies perfectly straight to align her spine
to the tree of life. Oh with words, she has such a way!
Even her pajama seams are perfectly aligned!
Fingers and toes and sacrum and mind!
She is a body prayer, breathing the name of God.
Inhale. Exhale. Inhale. Exhale. God's true name is spoken
as my mother aligns her spine to complete the day.

Now I too align myself with that great wisdom tree.
The one promised to me. The one connected
to the very truth root that sets us free.
I don't know the name of God my mother knows.
I just imagine her, breathing it for me. Inhale. Exhale.
Mothers do that you know, moderating our life flow.
Breathe for their babies in their red womb home.
Lady Mary did it for her itty bitty baby tree.
Born to help the blind to see. But do we?

They say the apple doesn't fall far from the tree.
Oh! How I wish that was more true for me,
because my mother is the wisest woman on earth.
According to me. She is so very kind to me.
She is dynamic combination of delight and severity
teaching me the view from the fence, or the tree.
With her camel bags packed with the Holy Word
and ancient remedy and the Kabbalah of our mothers
she leads our flock to safety.

I praise you and thank you my
Good Mother and Good Father Creator,
for a good mother, a poet! Blessed Be!
She heeds the call of the Master in naming me
for what she hoped I would become.
I pray for her sake alone, that I be a good apple!
Thy will be done!
Perhaps if I am good, even an apple of *your* eye!
I shall do my best to serve you
as my mother taught me, I'll try!

Born This Way

I am the daughter of a
poet and a pirate
so is it any wonder
I turned out this way?

My mother says
the morning I was
born, the sun and the full
moon were in the sky
at the same time
and the mimosa tree
tree was blooming outside
the window where
I first yelled out to life.

I have been a rebel
since I could think
for myself and since a child,
I have not ceased to stand for justice.

I am most comfortable
in the spaces between
the spaces
at peace in the paradox
and so I decided as early
as I could I would
be an artist even if I
didn't know how to make
art worthy of winning any prizes.

I left art school for the hills
danced naked in the woods
howled at the moon
and bled into the earth
and called it good.

My image came and found
me one day in the shape of
an egg and I have worked
for her ever since.

If I was not concerned
with what my mother would think
my body would be
covered in tattoos
of roses and thorns
and sacred hearts
with fire cores and
tiny crosses of hope,
marking my skin -
rays of light coming
out everywhere.

When I am old,
I shall have a Mohawk
and combat boots
and as the days progress,
I am certain I will find
my way to my wildest self.
I could only hope to be considered notorious.
When I am rocking in my chair
with kittens and little ones gathered,

I shall tell them:
I lived as if I was living
instead of living
as if I was dying.
I am not even close
to being done
with all there is to create.

Some call me mystic,
art doctor, den mother,
chief laughing cloud
of the Cosmic Cowgirls.
I know one of my gifts
is moving at the speed of light
when gravity presses me down
I push up with wonder woman strength
I am sure the Virgin Mary
assigned to me special powers
because of all the stuff
she wanted to put
on my 'to do' list.
My mother said
I was born this way.
I only know I woke up today
and wanted to grow up to be a poet
whether or not I am worthy
of such grand name as 'poet'.

LANTERNS FROM THE ISLE OF LEWIS

My Lover

finding the song
the
Beloved

CHAPTER 10

Dear Reader,

Most of these poems are written after meeting my now husband, Jonathan. They didn't want to be woven in with everything else. Not because they are so very different or because I am, but because it was from a different time frame of my life and experience. And following the heaviness and personal stories I just shared with you, these seemed light enough to complete in love.

This collection starts off with one very magical poem, a poem I wrote to call Jonathan, my Beloved, to me. There are parts of it that are so magical. On our first date, I gave him the draft of this book of poetry to read, and asked him to choose one, he chose, 'A Note to My Future Lover.' And I tell you true, it is our story and his favorite color is yellow. Ask me to tell you sometime about the glass of wine that ended up in the painting of the yellow heart. Yes, love can come again. I didn't believe it could, but it did and I am ever so grateful.

Most of the café's I have now are with him and so some of the poems are not love poems in the regular sense, but rather, inspirations that arose from our conversations. Those sacred quantum conversations that happen in the wee hours of the morning when my Muse and his settle in for a that cup of coffee by candlelight.

Signed in yellow roses and white wedding lace,
Shiloh Sophia

A Note to My Future Lover

I don't want to live a life
without you looking at me in awe.
Without me looking at you and marveling
at the freckle where God kissed your cheek.
I don't want to live each day
without you noticing the curl
that has escaped my braids.
Without me, seeing you across a table
and wondering just who you really are.
I don't want to spend my days
not seeing your fragile power as your magic.
Without me feeding you chocolate on a hot day.
I want to live in splendor.
In fire. In water. In hearth. In winged air.
I want to breathe possibility.
I want to see the color yellow, truly, each time
and point it out to you.
You will have already noticed it.
I want your breath to remind me
of God breathing us from soil into light.
I want to take vibrancy in as medicine for the spirit.
I want the soul's organs to spin brightly
with aliveness and adventure.
I want to tell stories to you.
I want you to feed yours to me like hot plums.
Sometimes I want it sweet, sometimes hot.
I want to lie beneath fronded branches,
noticing the greening light
making patterns on your skin.

I want to make altars everywhere I go
and include things from your pockets.
Lint. A coin. Some matches. A rosary.
A tiny love note. A small white stone.
Anything will do, so long as it has belonged to you.
Every day is sacred if we choose for it to be.
I don't want to be asleep.
I don't want to miss anything.
And I want to have as many kisses
as I feel like having. Okay?
I want to know what you want. Truly.
This is what is important to me.
Do you think I am asking too much?
Perhaps.
At least if I know what I want
my longing will not go unexpressed.
I want a lover who will glow in the dark
so I can find my way to you.

I am calling you now.
I feel you near.
Can you hear me?

Being Available to Grace

There is a sacred space held inside
from the time when we are little.
When we are finally ready to wake up,
as we grow up,
we get to take a look within.
If we are really ready to see
the beauty that is there,
we can bring it with us.
This is a blessed journey.
Our inner world begins a conscious journey
into our outer world.
Eventually over time and with astonishment . . .
and intimacy with the details
there is an integration
between the two worlds.
An experience
of coming home to ourselves.
This is the day
we are all waiting for
even though we might not know that is
what we have been seeking all along.
We didn't forget who we are,
and we aren't just remembering lost selves.
We are becoming ourselves.
This takes time. And intention.
Once we are awakened,
we feel everything, often too much.
This awakeness at times is wearisome.
But when we use our gifts of creativity

and self expression
we learn to navigate the space
rich with so much sensation.
Then, there is a quiet joy that begins
to emerge, to rise up.
This quiet joy will
carry us through the deepest waters.
This buoyancy isn't something we earn,
but something we learn.
Grace comes. Gratitude comes.
We come to life!
Making ourselves available to grace.

I am Ready to Love You

Say to your body
I am sorry I haven't listened
more closely to your messages.
I am ready to love you.

Say to your heart
I am sorry for not asking
what you really felt.
I am ready to love you.

Say to your mind
I am sorry I haven't taken the time
to get to know how you work.
I am ready to love you.

Say to your soul
I am sorry it has taken so long,
but I am here now.
I am ready to love you.

Say to the Divine
Thank you for giving me this temple,
a luscious and luminous house for my spirit.
I am ready to love you.

Inner Lanterns

Our shadows are our inner lanterns
Showing us what we are not seeing
Our hollowed out places make space
Revealing where we haven't been listening
Our edges reveal the depth of our experience
Cutting away that which has blocked true feeling
Our demons that we have wrestled with so long
Transform our judgments of others into compassion
Our unwillingness to live our most vibrant colorful self
Will eventually dissolve into unbridled self expression
Our hidden desires and unspeakable stories
Become the transcendent material of freedom
This is what happens when we make art
When we draw the red thread right from the heart
For this we praise the Creative One
In whose image we are made to create

Sheltering Forest

There are places on my bark
Where the moss doesn't cover over
The green life that grows falters and parts
Your refuge shelters the tender places
Between the mosses and the gloaming lichens
You stroke gently the roughness in between
My roots unshaken quiver in accord
With the attention you pay to each branch
As if it was the whole of me holy
At the highest point, where I reach for sky
Your upward gaze affirms my direction
I don't have to wonder where I am headed anymore
You are the deepest blue aqua cenote
A cleft in the hard stone of the hill of this life
A deep place where I can dive in and downward
Within your pattern of witness
My growing cycle commences
Beauty ensues in astonishing arcs
To be known the way you choose to know me
To be in the space of sacred ground
Within your sheltering forest
My heart is a green thing growing
Shoots sprouting up from dry ground
As the rain comes, I see you looking up
You give thanks
I give thanks
We live in the thankfulness
of green growing

Waiting for You Since Forever

I am star struck with love
spinning in possibility
I want to light up the sky
I want to evolve slowly and quickly
I don't want to stay as I was before
I want to become me by becoming me
not waiting around for validation or approval
I want to take up the space that is mine
without apology or introduction
I want to make space for your big brightness
because we share this cosmic sky
If people don't bring you vitality
don't invite them for tea anymore
Choose those who want to light the sky
with you and share their stories
I am star struck with your beauty
and I can tell you are with mine
Let's light this place with hearts of fire
and psalms of praise for the Beloved
Meet me at the tree of togetherness
because there is a sacred happening there
and I know we belong together
I have been waiting for you
since from forever

Oysters and Champagne for Mermaids

You beckoned the mermaids to come
to the opening at the cave door.
You promised kipper snacks.
They didn't answer at first
but continued to watch their favorite sitcom.
They could hear you but said nothing.
when you couldn't find the cave opening.
You said it wasn't your fault.
They said, We know,
but we have waiting for a long time.
Come back another day.

You came back another day.
This time still with kippers but you added
Champers and oysters. A wise move.
They are suckers for pearls and
Love to spend the afternoon picking
opal shells apart with their teeth
searching for pearls to adorn themselves with.

They could smell the oysters across the waves.
One combed her blonde locks
Another one turned on some music
and started to dance.
But the wildest one swam to the opening
and saw you waiting quizzically on the rock.
She blindfolded you and you said nothing.
She brought you inside.
You were amazed at what you beheld.

They stormed you for your oysters
and your fishes.

They let you stay all night.

You were never the same.
Neither were the mermaids
because now they wait for you,
leaving you seaweed snacks on
various rocks throughout your life.

The song of the salty sailors and
laughing mermaids has become
the name tattooed on your bicep.
They will follow you anywhere now.

p.s. don't forget!
we like anchovies on our pizza

Intimacy with the Universe

If you knew how it really is
You would have quiet conversations
with everything that is
That ancient tree bark
has waited for your touch
That flaming hot pink coral colored flower
has anticipated your amazed gaze
That succulent stinking sweet fruit
has been expecting your surprised tongue
That shimmery star at night
shines on your upturned face
That sun in magenta streaked morn
bathes your body in brightness
That aqua ocean lit up from within
rushes to meet your expectant body
Those stones anticipate your
sitting upon them to ponder
That chocolate pearl
presents herself to your kiss
Who knows for how long
this waiting has been going on?
The island sounds your name
You wonder, how could she know?
She knows, and now you know
You are never really alone

Everything that is
Is responding to you
responding to it

We are a constellation of witnesses
who have barely begun to see
each other for who we are
Perhaps it is just too much
for us to bear, knowing how
everything is awake but us?
Eventually if we walk softly
and listen to the humming with new ears
and choose to have eyes that open to wonder
we will come alive
She is showing us how

COMPLETING THE CIRCLE

Sharing my mom with you

Here you will find my mother Caron's answer to the question, 'Where Are You From' inspired by the poet, *George Ella Lyon*. **I was moved by her writings here and felt since the volume is dedicated to her you might want to see what she is up to in her story.**

Tears, Laughter and Fencing
By Caron McCloud
Fence II:

"Where are you from?"
Asked this question in my youth
I would have said:
I come from laughter and from tears.
I come from a long line of Gypsies
who live and dance on the edges of your worlds.
And if invited, I may move beyond my fences
into your house,
as though I am going to stay forever.
And if welcome, with sage and prayer and chantings
I will drive out the devils of seven sorrows,
and with sacred oil,
I will bless and seal your arches and gateways,
your door posts from lintel to threshold.
I will repair your broken shingles,
patch, paint and paper your faded walls.
I will clean and make paisley curtains
for your windows, and seal their sills, also.
I will cook consecrated chicken soup for you,
and the best damned spaghetti you've ever had.
I will build you a book case and fill it with stories.

I will write you stories and I will read you stories.
And come bedtime, I will tuck you in.
I will hold you in my arms and rock you,
singing lullabies and love songs.
I will dry your tears and I will make you laugh.
I will buy you a little red truck and a pony,
a violin and dancing shoes.
I will dance with you. I will dance for you.
Barefoot. And you may have your way with me.

I will wind your clocks and wash your socks,
clean your closets and rescue
your ancestor's captured moments from
old trunks in the attic, your children's
from shoeboxes in drawers,
frame them, and hang them on your walls,
so you can remember who you are.
I will plant you a garden.
And I will write you a poem
so you will remember who I am.

But don't get too attached.
I may be only passing through.
And if you hurt me, or mine,
you will come home one day
and I will be gone. Gone,
without even a message
in red lipstick written on the mirror.
I will be gone. Gone beyond the fence
I have built for you. Gone in tears.
Gone in search of laughter.

And you may ask yourself . . .
What is that beautiful house?

And you may ask yourself . . .
Where does that highway go to?

And you may ask yourself . . .
Am I right? . . .Am I wrong?

And you may say to yourself
My God! . . .What have I done?!

- Talking Heads, Once in a Lifetime

List of Illustrations

By Shiloh Sophia

Learning to See in the Light

Queen of Her Own Heart - Chapter 1

Tending the Sacred Flame - Chapter 2

The Legend Lives in Her Heart - Chapter 3

Enter the Heart - Chapter 4

Key to the House of the Heart - Chapter 5

Molting My Archetype - Chapter 6

Chief Soul Fire - Chapter 7

Heart of the Visionary - Chapter 8

Born This Way - Chapter 9

Song of the Beloved - Chapter 10

Divine Lullaby - Closing the Circle

About Shiloh Sophia

Guiding those she works with to release and re-examine societal, familial and personal conditioning is the seed of Shiloh Sophia's life work and the inspiration for this material, Tea with the Midnight Muse.

The content of the book will not be surprising to anyone familiar with her work, as since her early years she has acted a rebel in resistance of the dominant paradigm. She wrote her first poetry, as a teen in her diary, about feeling captured and caged by societal norms. Her imagination expressed in writing and drawing was to become her medicine of choice to survive and provide an antidote for herself and others.

Her first little flock in high school was called the Rage Club and would bring together the geeks, punks, gays and outcasts to organize around being who they were, without apology. She invited those close to her to create themselves and invent their own way through. And above all, examine, and if needed, reject what is expected of you by others, all so that you can reveal you to yourself.

Her philosophy of survival, and ultimately thriving, through creativity is an invitation to a quest to become more and more of one's self, and a rebellion against whatever is currently deemed normal or standard or accepted paradigm.

"Dominant conformity frameworks change from age to age but never cease to dominate us until we are conscious of the invisible pressure it imposes." This domination, what she has affectionately and with candor coined, *"Surviving the attack of the beige people,"* has been a catalyst for her work with poetry, prose and paintings. It was clear to her from an early age

that fitting in was what would cost her everything that was precious and unique. Being an outcast meant freedom, albeit a sometimes lonely sentence.

"I live with an unreasonable hope that we might think for ourselves. My sacred assignment is to guide others to access their internal information. This happens through acts of intentional creativity. It is all within us, some of us just call it out. See there — see that cosmic portal, jump in there, and see what's going on."

Shiloh Sophia believes that when we encounter others who have access to 'their own information' and are aware of it, we can get sparked and inspired in our own paths through contact with them and their work. These are often the ones who are predisposed towards the condition, or diagnosis of a 'creative:' poets, painters, musicians, dancers, actors, dissidents. Being with them or their work, something in us remembers, and calls us forward. *"When we answer the call, the real movement of awakening begins and the path begins to reveal itself, in front of us. Where there once was no path, now we are called forward by a force greater than we knew was in there, but was within us all along - our own unique voice. This is holy ground."*

As she developed her writing and painting, she began to see the impact it could have on others and she was, as it were, called forward. She had a fixation on people not only having access to themselves, but accessibility to the points of access she found most useful: painting, drawing and writing. Not some high and mighty version of poetry and paint that from its loft becomes unavailable to the untrained eye or ear. Rather something that could almost pass as normal and therefore sneak through to the ones who may need it the most and unsuspectingly wake them from their slumber. To those who may have thought they had no use of poetry or painting, material could be the opening to a creative self who holds the keys to freedom.

Creativity provided early success for Shiloh Sophia in her twenties. Having a sold out show of illuminated poems, photography, paintings and pottery, she found a place to stand which she could call her own, as an artist. A year prior to the show, she had left art academia, *"I dropped out of art school, feeling one day like I had nothing to draw, at the time having no idea that every image I truly sought was within me. They didn't teach that there, and I was terrified by my revelation that there was nothing left to draw in San Francisco. No one told me all the good stuff is inside the inner landscape of the soul. I had to discover that on my own, but once I did, I found it was already all around me; the very matrix from which I was woven was made from the stuff of what was inside. However, the language that would tell me where to look remained hidden, tattoos waiting to be revealed on the skin of the inside self."*

Under the tutelage of her teachers, Caron McCloud, the Poetry Mother, and Sue Hoya Sellars, the Art Mother, she took to the hills and explored finding what she called her Mother Tongue, with the two women who parented her and encouraged her to, *"Be creative at all costs, including fitting in."* An airstream trailer on the mountaintop and a chop wood, carry water mentorship with Sue Hoya Sellars would become just the fuel needed to stoke the young artist's fire. The sparks of the Intentional Creativity Movement would be lit and begin a blaze that would guide her life until now, and that of thousands and thousands of women, and the men who love them.

For Shiloh Sophia as the work unfolded it became clearer and clearer that it was much more than making art, but a philosophy and life path. Art making isn't just for art sake, but for liberation and justice making. For four years in a row her tribe has travelled to the United Nations to bring the work of Intentional Creativity into the arena of human rights. *"Self expression is a basic human right, the capacity to know and have access to one's own story."*

Her explorations of image, language and the feminine, specifically the Blessed Mother and Wisdom Sophia, in those formative years would be the foundation upon which she would build the rest of her life work, what she calls her sacred assignment and would inform her work with women.

In addition to writing and painting as an entrepreneur, Shiloh Sophia was one of the top grossing artists in the United States for over ten years. *"I didn't see a movement that I wanted to be a part of that felt how this kind of working feels, so I decided to make one up. All movements start out that way; if we are honest, they are moving a body of work to a new place along the path of creative evolution as understood by both the artists and the viewers, and their critics and supporters. When it reaches even a small number of people in which a philosophy of creation is employed, then it can become a movement. We certainly have that. We call it the Intentional Creativity Movement. We didn't start it; ancients started it with all art created in a sacred manner. Since the beginning of time, creating with intention has been alive. We are just beginning to see how truly quantum it can be and how it can work on becoming conscious."*

Her early work with her peers, combined with her heart for healing women and ending violence and suffering of all kinds, would eventually become the inspiration to call together a group of wild women called the Cosmic Cowgirls who ride through the cosmos together to transform their own lives into legends. *"We are edge-riders. We live between worlds embracing the paradox."*

"From the space of being empowered in our own story, we then can move forward to bring our love out to others. We are born to love; the question is if we can get free enough from our existing stories to love, and love what it is we truly love. And then, guided by that love, act."

In Tea with the Midnight Muse we find a collection of writings, inquiries and guided mini-quests that invite the reader to journey to their own sacred space where she teaches that the Muse dwells.

She has volumes of teachings on creativity, but one of her most beloved teachings is about the critic. The critic, that voice in our heads often showing up as the tyrant, can be transformed into our ally; however, it must be courted into personal transformation. But how, one might wonder, do we transform that dominant jailor we are so familiar with that we scarcely know it even exists, into something that is useful or that serves us? Can the predator become an ally?

"The critic often manifests as the accumulated voices, ties, cages, societal, religious or familial norms and frames to which we are to adhere, but at the cost of the individual voice of our soul. Our own unique self atrophies, and the critic rages on. We, as human beings, need something to work with, to create with, something that is our own, or we go rather mad. To speak to one's self as if we are not enough or cannot get this right is its own form of madness that has greater implications than we can imagine: a world of beings who are disconnected from themselves and their hearts."

She says transforming our voice has everything to do with courting the Muse, who is the antidote and sometimes fickle animator of that voice. Yes, that same mechanism that has told us we are worthless, sometimes from the time we are seven to eight years old, with care and creation can now show us where our own magic has its dwelling place. Access is granted once again to the place many of us left as a child, to be resumed at some later date, which for many never comes.

The Muse shows us how to venture forth and gather the fragmented stories from the field, far and wide, that surround our very bodies and stitch them back together.

"My writings are probes from the muse" states Shiloh Sophia. *"Not attempts at the great halls of poetry, but more like recipes that lead to something yummy at the end of our labors in some familiar café where we like to hang out. I like them to be understandable and to work instantly, if at all possible, like taking down a curtain to reveal a landscape that has always been there."*

Her early spiritual roots found her on a mystical path, once ordained as reverend and deacon in the independent sacramental movement. She has, for the time being, taken off her mantle and employs the paintbrush and pen as her sacramental offering. Hers is a call to service, which one will find as a repeated pattern in these pages. She has passed on her teachings and the teachings of her of Intentional Creativity lineage through Caron McCloud, Sue Hoya Sellars, and before her, Lenore Thomas Straus, through a certification teacher training called Color of Woman. The graduates form the global Guild of Intentional Creatives.

Shiloh Sophia considers herself to be part of creating a planet that truly works, where people are free to be who they are instead of who society or the system has created them out to be. *"Peace will not come from agreement of belief, but from the freedom to believe differently, and still be able to stand together."*

She has written and illustrated many books, teaches worldwide, and has a classroom where she teaches and gathers women in Northern California. She dwells in the beautiful wine country and oceans of the Sonoma Coast, with her husband, Jonathan, also a poet, teacher and chef. Together, they run a boutique inn, museum and school called MUSEA.

They also travel the world, teaching in Paris, Italy, Denmark and beyond teaching the wild wisdom of creativity and quantum physics.

"Muse is code language for the hidden self, the one that teaches us to think for ourselves and who knows the keys to let ourselves out of our own cages. Without this awareness we may find ourselves lost, or worse, asleep. I am into the work of waking up, and then getting down to what matters, to answering to what calls us. If we aren't awake and find ourselves numb to the world and to our own hearts, we will continue to allow the dominant culture to direct our futures. And that clearly isn't working."

In Tea with the Midnight Muse, the reader is called into action, not as a passive observer, but as a witness that becomes awakened to their own mysterious call rising from within.

Will you dare to encounter your Muse?

Acknowledgements & Gratitude

Thank you to my editors and friends who helped craft this book. Specifically, Caron McCloud, who first gave me poetry and helped me pull the first poems together.

Thank you for my friends and family who took the time to edit it for me and with me: Caron McCloud, Isabella Vickers, Samantha Bennett, Effy Wild, Leslie Nolan, Misty Frederick Ritz, Barbara Hall, Jeri Brady, Trish O'Malley, Jennifer Russell, Wendy Hassel, Mary MacDonald and Jonathan Lewis.

SUPER DUPER Gratitude to my friends who have believed in me and supported my work and read it out loud, Elizabeth Gibbons, Christine Arylo, Amy Ahlers, Shannon Thompson, Sherri Morris, Heidi Damata, Julie Lampros, Susan Estes, D'vorah Grenn, Grace Steenberg, Havi Mandell, Sarah Mardell and Norma Jeanne Maloney. Thank you to my cousin Bridget, my Aunt Janet and my sister Shannon for being the Grant Girls with me. And my little sister Laurel for our deep Davis roots. Big love to Jimmie, Bing, my step father who believed in my work from the beginning, took my first serious art class and never stopped painting from that day on! Gratitude to my first life partner, Rahm Isaiah who was also one of my greatest teachers and taught me how to be strong in adversity, to define my path, and speak my truth. The first poems were written in your company. To my Grandmas, Eden McCloud and Helen Davis for taking the time they took with me to shape me into who I am. I would also like to thank Alice Walker and Judy Grahn, womanist mentors in the realm of poetry whose work showed me contrast, long view vision and insight. Special love goes to Dr. Clarissa Pinkola Estes whose works sparked a revolution for wild women.

Special gratitude to my United Nations Social Art Activist Social Justice mentors, Lys Anzia of WNN and Lois Herman of Women's United Nations Report Network – WUNRN.

Thank you for my husband, Jonathan Lewis, who has been helping me bring this to this moment of sharing, and inspired the last poems this book needed. And has created such a powerful context for our lives to happen in. And yes, has sat through many, many readings of many of these poems.

Thank you for all of you who have asked for this book to come into form so that you could use them in your own lives and circles. Thank you for appreciating my writing, and letting me know that you did. I was always writing to you. For you. I was always having tea with you, in the Red Thread Café.

In my work I feel I am called forward by those I am here to serve, my students and Beloveds, and this book and work is so very much about you and for you and inspired by you. I love you.

Thank you to my painting mentor, Sue Hoya Sellars, who taught me how to see and find narrative from my paintings. Yes, they do speak.

Thank you, mentor of my mentor, Lenore Thomas Straus for showing Sue, who showed me, what it means to bring image, language and inquiry together.

Thank you to the Cosmic Cowgirls, especially Mary MacDonald and Jenafer Owen, for walking with me through close to ten years of these writings, for your friendship and faith in the work.

Thank you to my Muse, she who lives within, and lights the path and shows me where to find the jewels in the shadows.

Thank you to this sacred earth and all creation. Praise to the Great Creator and the Blessed Lady and my Yeshua for giving me such an inspirational well from which to draw living water.

And to the Universe. This sacred design. Earth. Air. Fire. Water. Star. Cosmos. May my 'sack of stars' serve the great unfolding. Here I am.

Shiloh Sophia

Other Books by the Author

Color of Woman

She Moves To Her Own Rhythm

Her Evolution

She Dances Between the Worlds

On A Wing and A Dream

Way of the Red Thread

Heart of the Visionary – Co-Authored with the Cosmic Cowgirls

Illustrated Publications

Hard Times Require Furious Dancing – Illustrator with Author Alice Walker

Mother Mary Oracle – Illustrator with Author Alana Fairchild

Mending Invisible Wings – Illustrator with Author Mary Burgess

Photo by Jonathan Lewis
Shiloh Sophia

Artist. Poet. Curator. Revolutionary.

I am Shiloh Sophia. I have always been a rebel, while at the same time dedicated to the sacred. I have walked both worlds for a long time. My mom said I was born this way. There is something in me that won't stay still. I write poetry and paint paintings to keep myself from going too wild in the world while at the same time making sure I do. Not that going wild isn't what's called for; it's just that there are things that need tending, like hearts that I care for in this world, my Beloveds.

Sometime in my early twenties, I left my cushy, corporate downtown San Francisco life of high heels and martinis and headed for the hills, as in the mountains of Terra Sophia where the art matriarch Sue

Hoya Sellars lived. There, I let go of my beliefs and patterns and gods I had named and began to explore who I might be without my 'story.'

Well, if you have ever tried that, you know you just make up more stories. So I started to voraciously paint and to write poetry, to work with clay, and expand my awareness of being. I wanted to discover what story wanted to live in me and I have been living some version of my own personal made up legend ever since. Unweaving and reweaving as a way of being, I became an artist.

I have always been surrounded by art, as my mother Caron was my first art teacher. When I was a child she would draw for me images of beautiful fashionable ladies that I would color. This was one of my favorite things to do and greatly influenced my style, and what I call "the curve of my line."

Yep, this being an artist, it's a dangerous territory set up for those who are willing to dare to explore themselves and who they might be. Creating art is legend making. I mean, it worked for me. So women come and paint and pray with me, and some of them even like what I teach them enough to teach it to others . . . *supremely humble coolness factor. This is what I love – seeing the beauty accessible to others.*

I have every intention of continuing to create books and poems because it is why I am excited to wake up every day. At the heart of my work is the desire to end suffering; that is my personal piece of the red thread and I tend that piece through intentional creativity.

It sounds lofty crazy, huh? Each day I can get up and work to end suffering through adding a brush stroke of red roses into women's hair, painting Madonnas, extending red threads to others and through the gathering of bones and stones to make poetry.

"How," one might ask, "does this end suffering?"
Poets and artists know the answer, but I will
leave you with this question anyway.

What or who is it that you wake up to serve?

Find the answer to that question and you discover how painting and
poetry does its fair share to end suffering.

Let's Connect Our Red Threads

Shiloh Sophia
www.shilohsophia.com

This book
www.teawiththemidnightmuse.com

Our community and education
www.cosmiccowgirls.com

May Love Be at The Center of All Choices

If you no longer need this book, leave it in the full moonlight and it will either self destruct or the Muses will come and retrieve it for fire starting in someone else's heart. In gratitude, thank you for joining me and my Midnight Muse for Tea in the Red Thread Café.

Printed in the United States
By Bookmasters